THE AMERICAN AS REFORMER

The American as Reformer

ARTHUR M. SCHLESINGER

HARVARD UNIVERSITY PRESS
Cambridge, Massachusetts
1950

This study was made possible through the financial assistance received from the John Randolph Haynes and Dora Haynes Foundation, a charitable and educational trust organized "for the purpose of promoting the well-being of mankind." The interpretation of the data and the judgments expressed are the views of the author rather than of the Foundation.

Distributed in Great Britain by Geoffrey Cumberlege Oxford University Press, London

Printed in the United States of America

Is it not the glory of the people of America, that, whilst they have paid a decent regard to the opinions of former times and other nations, they have not suffered a blind veneration for antiquity, for custom, or for names, to overrule the suggestions of their own good sense, the knowledge of their own situation, and the lessons of their own experience? . . . Had no important step been taken by the leaders of the Revolution for which a precedent could not be discovered, no government established for which an exact model did not present itself, the people of the United States might, at this moment, be numbered among the melancholy victims of misguided councils, must at best have been laboring under the weight of some of those forms which have crushed the liberties of the rest of mankind.

James Madison in *The Federalist*, no. 14 (1787).

Unquestioning idolatry of the status quo *has never been an American characteristic.*

Justice Robert H. Jackson's Opinion in American Communications Association *v.* Douds (1950).

CONTENTS

FOREWORD

In his essay, "History and the Reader," G. M. Tre-velyan, the distinguished British historian, reminds us that individuals cannot understand their "own personal opinions, prejudices and emotional reactions" unless they possess a knowledge of their nation's history.[1] To which it may be added that in times of public emotion and confusion a whole people can find light and guidance by an intelligent examination of its past.

The United States enters the second half of the twentieth century in a state of national confusion unparalleled for many years. No people ever had greater need of the Delphic injunction, "Know Thyself." Professor Schlesinger's interpretation of one aspect of our past is a guide to sanity and stability. In swift strokes he presents the reformer and his opponents in action, throwing much light on the major conflicts of our history since the movement for national independence. Scholar and general reader alike will find new viewpoints and stimulating analyses of many crises of the American past.

Through the importance of the United States in world affairs, our history has acquired a universal

[1] *An Autobiography and Other Essays* (London, 1949).

quality. Professor Schlesinger's volume is in the broad
tradition in which all future American history must
be written. One senses in his pages the story of a nation now taking its place with Rome, Spain, France,
and Britain among the states which have profoundly
influenced human thought and action. Conscious of
the position our land has attained, Professor Schlesinger warns us against false or cheap appeals in the
name of America and Americanism. "To the historian," he says, "such fevers and fears evidence a sorry
lack of faith in American ideals and in the capacity
of free institutions to command the people's continuing confidence and allegiance."

The lectures out of which this volume grew were
delivered at Pomona College, Claremont, California,
in the spring of 1950, when Professor Schlesinger
held the John Randolph Haynes and Dora Haynes
Foundation Lectureship. The Haynes Foundation of
Los Angeles, established by a liberal and civic-minded
California physician and his wife, is one of the most
significant regional foundations in America today.
Dedicated to study and research in economic, political, and social questions in the Los Angeles area, it is
giving remarkable leadership to a new and phenome-
nally expanding region. In close association with the
institutions of higher learning in Southern California,
it has sponsored a program of publishing which has
provided invaluable and otherwise unprocurable

studies in the fields of local government, economic development, and labor relations. To its already great services the Haynes Foundation in 1949 added an annual lectureship on some important problems of contemporary American life. The privilege of presenting the lectures is awarded to the colleges and universities of the Los Angeles region. Pomona College was honored to be chosen as the sponsor in 1950.

Readers of this book, and may they be many across the country, will see at once why Professor Schlesinger's lectures made such a profound impression on his audiences in Southern California. Foreigners will find in *The American as Reformer* a brilliant interpretation of much that is most American. Our own citizens will acquire deep understanding of how and why we have changed our institutions from generation to generation. Such understanding will be wise counsel in the greatest period of change our country has ever known.

E. Wilson Lyon

Claremont, California
June 19, 1950

THE HISTORICAL CLIMATE
OF REFORM

1

THE HISTORICAL CLIMATE
OF REFORM

"I wish to offer to your consideration some thoughts on the particular and general relations of man as a reformer." Ralph Waldo Emerson thus opened a famous address in 1841 on the first great upsurge of social reform in United States history. At the time American society along the seaboard was two centuries old. The people had subdued the savages, reshaped their physical environment, won political independence, established representative institutions, founded towns and cities, developed agriculture and trade, entered upon manufacturing. The country had attained a provisional maturity, and despite the more primitive conditions on the western frontier, thinking men were taking stock of the achievements and conducting what the speaker called a "general inquisition into abuses." And so, as Emerson went on to say, "In the history of the world the doctrine of Reform had never such scope as at the present hour." It seemed to him that every human institution was being questioned—"Christianity, the laws, commerce, schools, the farm, the laboratory"—and that not a "town, statute, rite, calling, man, or woman, but is threatened by the new spirit." [1]

A hundred years afterward, Emerson's words sound as if they had been uttered of our own age, though whether the spirit of reform be deemed a threat or promise is a matter of personal opinion, and Emerson's other remarks attest that he himself regarded it as vital to social health. Between his time and ours of course much has happened. Cycles of reform and repose have come and gone until by a giant turn of the wheel the American people again find themselves in a period when in the history of the world the doctrine of reform had never such scope as at the present hour. In venturing to treat Emerson's theme a century later I need hardly say that I do so without Emerson's intuitive wisdom and philosophic acumen. Instead, I bring to it the poorer gifts of the historical scholar, those of the foot soldier rather than of the air pilot. I can only hope that the longer span of national experience since his day, plus the historian's special approach, will add something, however slight, to an understanding of the conditions and nature of the reform impulse in the United States.

I

The reform urge has obviously not been an American monopoly, nor has the nation ever been immune to struggles for human betterment elsewhere. In particular there has been a like-mindedness with England. The colonists were deeply indebted to the mother country for their notions of individual liberty and free institutions, as well as for that "salutary neglect" —Burke's phrase—which enabled them to develop these conceptions yet farther. Even after Independence this kinship continued, as it has to the present time. Ideologically America has never been isolated from Europe nor Europe from America, and the cross-fertilization of ideals and practices has yielded mutual benefit.[2]

The United States, however, until very recent times has nearly always set the pace for the Old World in reform zeal. The outstanding exception has been in solutions for the social maladjustments arising from industrialization, where Britain as the older country faced these problems in acute form before America was hardly aware of them. The English, for example, led in factory legislation, the mitigation of child labor and the legalizing of trade-unions. Another but less conclusive instance in a different field was England's earlier abolition of Negro servitude. The two governments, obeying a common impulse, acted simultaneously in 1807 to outlaw the African slave trade; then Britain ended human bondage throughout the Empire in 1833, whereas the United States waited until 1865. This delay was not due to any lack of will on the part of American humanitarians, however, but to the fact that the circumstances in the two lands were so very different. In England's case the institution existed some thousands of miles away. Moreover, Parliament had full power to deal with it, and the colonies affected were in a static or decaying economic condition. In America, on the other hand, slavery not only existed at home, but it was anchored in state and local law and was recognized by the Federal Constitution. It was also bound up, directly or indirectly, with the material welfare of a large part of the nation. Nonetheless Britain's action inspired the immediate formation of the American Anti-Slavery Society and so threw the American movement into higher gear.

In the case of most other social innovations, however, America has stood at the forefront. Thus (white) manhood suffrage was attained in the United States by the middle of the nineteenth century but not in England until the early twentieth. In like manner America outstripped the older country in regard to liberty of the press, the separation of church and state, the abolition of barbarous punishments, restraints on the liquor traffic, public education and prison reform, not to mention other achievements.

II

The basic reason for the generally faster pace of reform may be found in two conditions. In the first place, men were not burdened to the same extent by the weight of tradition. Less energy had to be used in tearing down the old and revered, more was left for building anew, and the large measure of self-government enjoyed even by the colonists simplified the process. As Emerson put it on one occasion,

America was opened after the feudal mischief was spent, and so the people made a good start. . . . No inquisition here, no kings, no nobles, no dominant church. . . . We began with freedom, and are defended from shocks now for a century by the facility with which through popular assemblies every necessary measure of reform can instantly be carried.[3]

The second factor was the kind of people who emigrated to America, not only the original settlers but also their successors, the far greater number of immigrants. Early or late, these transplanted Europeans were men who rebelled against conditions as they found them in their homelands—against a class society, against religious, political and economic oppression—and, unlike their more docile neighbors, they carried their rebellion to the point of going to a distant continent where life was strange, dangers abounded and new careers must be sought. The departure of such folk slowed down the impetus to change at home, just as it tended to quicken it in the adopted country.

Given these two circumstances, the surprising thing is that the tempo of reform in America was not far more precipitate. As Anthony Trollope observed with particular reference to the Revolutionary era, "this new people, when they had it in their power to change all their laws, to throw themselves upon any Utopian theory that the folly of a wild philanthropy could devise, . . . did not do so." [4] He attributed this caution to their inherited English practicality, but there was more to it than that. By starting life in a new state they acquired a new state of mind. Those who had fled from religious bigotry could now worship as they wished, those who had suffered political discrimination were generally free to vote and run for office, while all could make an easier living and attain a greater human dignity. To revise an old proverb, nothing sobers like success. The owner of property, however eager to improve society, has a personal investment in orderly change, and under conditions of self-government a legislative body is, as Emerson remarked in the essay just quoted, "a standing insurrection, and escapes the violence of accumulated grievance." [5]

In other words, virtually every newcomer to America underwent a sea change. No matter how desperate his lot had been in Europe, he quickly displayed what impatient extremists despise as a middle-class attitude toward reform. Being even surer of the future than of the present, he could not love innovation for its own sake, or be willing to risk all existing good in a general overturn. Hence he threw his weight on the side of piecemeal progress.

This temper has continued to dominate the American mind. Despite the growing industrialization and maldistribution of wealth of the last seventy-five years, despite the one third of the nation "ill-housed, ill-clad, ill-nourished," a Gallup poll a few years ago indicated that about nine out of every ten people still regard themselves as belonging to the great middle class.[6] This means, in contrast to most European countries, that there is no large self-conscious group which feels so inferior or so handicapped as not to be able to better itself by constitutional methods.

If this is an overstatement as regards the Negro, it is not so as regards the army of labor, whose leaders avoid the expression 'working class' because it implies permanent attachment to a status. American wage earners are, and always have been, capitalists on the make, and there are some observers who would say they have already arrived, since a number of the national unions possess bigger financial resources than many a college or university. The aggregate assets of all national and local labor organizations, including the funds for defense, pensions, welfare and other purposes, have recently been estimated at between three and four billion dollars.[7] The United Mine Workers, for example, whose president on a $50,000 salary looks, acts and lives like a 'robber baron' of the nineteenth century, help manage a miners' welfare fund increasing by $140,000,000 a year, and are able to contribute $420,000 to a national political campaign and offer million-dollar loans to other unions as well as to pay a court fine of $1,400,000.

The national preference for evolution over revolution, whether the revolution be peaceable or violent, has given the United States midway in the twentieth century the reputation abroad of being the last bulwark of conservatism. The kaleidoscopic disruptions of the two world wars have driven Europe to extreme measures of recovery and social reconstruction. By Communists the American method of progress is contemptuously dubbed 'bourgeois liberalism,' while even the democratic Socialists of Western Europe find little good in our way of making haste slowly.[8] Yet the mass of Americans remain unconvinced. In their own lifetime they have witnessed a Square Deal followed by a New Freedom followed by a New Deal and then a Fair Deal, each yielding social gains, and they know that the flame of reform burns as fiercely as ever and is as menacing to special privilege. Until events demonstrate the failure of this pragmatic approach, they may be counted upon not to try any different method.

Another historical factor working against headlong change has been freedom of speech and print. Practiced even in colonial times, it was enshrined in the basic law of the states and nation after the Revolution. Liberty of expression may not at first seem a moderating influence, since it is an open invitation to all malcontents to agitate their grievances. But that is just the point. For orderly progress it is better that crackpots rant in public than plot in private, and the very act, moreover, subjects their beliefs to comparison with the more constructive ideas of others. Only in this way can the critics be criticized, their proposals cut down to size, and an appropriate course be arrived at democratically.

Infringements on freedom of utterance almost invariably defeat their purpose either by attracting attention to the cause involved or by creating indignation over the denial of constitutional rights. For example, the murder of the abolitionist editor Elijah Lovejoy and the 'gag resolution' of the House of Representatives against antislavery petitions brought to the antislavery standard countless persons who had been unmoved by the woes of the Negro.[9] Our wisest conservatives have always understood this function of free speech. Alexander Hamilton, Daniel Webster, Charles E. Hughes and Wendell Willkie, to name no others, championed the liberty to express views which they themselves hated. Through this process of keeping the windows of discussion open, many a plausible reform has died of exposure, while others, more responsibly conceived, have won their way to public acceptance.

III

Whence has American reform derived its abiding vitality? Many rivulets have contributed to the stream, some with constant flow and others intermittently. None, however, has been more potent than religion. As Edmund Burke observed, "All Protestantism, even the most cold and passive, is a sort of dissent," but the men who settled the colonies represented "the dissidence of dissent and the Protestantism of the Protestant religion." [10]

Did this fact, however, always denote a general open-mindedness toward human rights and hopes? The Puritans, it has often been pointed out, though demanding freedom of conscience for themselves in England, denied it to others upon going to Massachusetts. But that is not the whole story. The core of Puritanism, once the theological husks are peeled away, was intense moral zeal both for one's own salvation and for that of the community. This attitude, as in the instance noted, could engender intolerance, but by the same token it could also engender intolerance of intolerance; and the history of the Puritan spirit as a social force in America shows that the disposition to challenge vested injustice was the more significant aspect.

Roger Williams and Anne Hutchinson are outstanding early examples. The New England clergymen who preached defiance of England as the Revolution approached exhibited the same quality in the political field. A Tory called them "Mr. Otis's black Regiment" who "like their Predecessors of 1641 . . . have been unceasingly sounding the Yell of Rebellion in the Ears of an ignorant & deluded people." [11] In like manner a later generation of the strain abetted most of the humanitarian crusades of Emerson's period, earning Bronson Alcott's affectionate encomium of being "the Lord's chore boys." [12] With equal ardor laymen of Puritan stock were at the same time promoting the public-school movement in New England and the newly settled West, thus enriching significantly the concept of democracy.

A similar concern for the public welfare galvanized most of the other religious groups. They too strove to comfort the afflicted and afflict the comfortable. In answer to protests against such activities a church-gathering in Peterboro, New York, resolved,

> That the correctness of this opinion turns wholly on the character of the politics which are preached: for whilst it is clearly wrong to preach anti-Bible or unrighteous politics on the Sabbath or on any other day, nothing can be clearer than that no day is too holy to be used in preaching the politics which are inculcated in the Bible. [13]

The Quakers in particular wielded an influence out of proportion to their numbers.

To be sure, the more breathless reformers sometimes rebuked the churches for faintheartedness, notably in the case of antislavery which created special difficulties by splitting the national bodies along sectional lines.[14] It is also true that the foes of reform, no less than the friends, resorted to the Bible for vindication. Not only the defenders of slavery but the opponents of temperance, of women's rights and of the peace movement managed to dig up scriptural authority. This, however, was something like the homage which vice pays to virtue, for the advantage rested inevitably with those who interpreted God as love, not as greed or oppression. Even the censorious William Lloyd Garrison was impressed when the two great popular churches, the Methodist and the Baptist, anticipated the political disruption of the Union by separating into Northern and Southern branches in 1844–1845 over a question involving slavery.

If America has been less ostensibly religious in more recent times, the teachings of Jesus have nevertheless continued as vitally to fuel humanitarian enterprises.[15] Churchgoers have been at the van of all such undertakings, and the clergy by espousing the 'social gospel' have opened minds to new human needs and persistently pricked the popular conscience. In short, religion, in America at least, has not been the opiate of the masses.

Even in politics liberal movements have turned constantly to Holy Writ for inspiration. William Jen-

nings Bryan in the greatest convention speech in
American history denounced the business magnates
who would press down upon the brow of labor a
"crown of thorns" and "crucify mankind upon a cross
of gold." Theodore Roosevelt, defying the reactionary leaders of the Republican party, declared he stood
at Armageddon and battled for the Lord. Woodrow
Wilson, a religionist in the Scottish Covenanter tradition, always kept his Bible by his bedside. And the
latest surge of political reform, the New Deal, took
as its slogan "the more abundant life." [16] President
Truman merely voiced a common opinion when he
declared in a recent address, our "belief in the dignity
and the freedom of man" is "derived from the word
of God, and its roots are deep in our spiritual foundations." [17]

IV

This belief, however, had independent support in
the doctrines derived from Europe's Age of Enlightenment. These eighteenth-century avowals of human
excellence and man's boundless capacity for progress
found instant and permanent lodgment in America,
where they confirmed common observation as well
as the more enlightened religious teachings. Incor-
porated in the Preamble of the Declaration of Independence, they not only served their immediate purpose, but resounded back to the Old World, where

they still reverberate. At home the Preamble was more a great editorial than a factual report, as none knew better than its slaveholding author Thomas Jefferson, but it proved an incomparable rallying cry for reformers then as it has ever since.

If all men are created equal, demanded the abolitionists in their day, why are black men held in bondage? If all are created equal, cried the feminists in their time, why are women denied their rights? If human beings are equally entitled to life, liberty and the pursuit of happiness, asked others in their turn, how justify the plight of the distressed farmers, underprivileged children, the hungry poor, the innocent victims of war? Not many years ago Roger Baldwin of the American Civil Liberties Union was arrested for attempting to read the Declaration of Independence in front of the City Hall during a labor outbreak in Paterson, New Jersey. However benighted the policeman's action may seem, he and his superiors should at least be given credit for recognizing the great manifesto as an irrefutable challenge to a repressive *status quo*.[18]

That indeed has been its historic function. No one has stated the case more tellingly in our own generation than a citizen of foreign birth.

If I ask an American [writes Mary Antin] what is the fundamental American law, and he does not answer me promptly, "That which is contained in the Declaration of

Independence," I put him down for a poor citizen. . . . What the Mosaic Law is to the Jews, the Declaration is to the American people. It affords us a starting-point in history and defines our mission among nations. . . . Up to the moment of our declaration of independence, our struggle with our English rulers did not differ from other popular struggles against despotic governments. Again and again we respectfully petitioned for redress of specific grievances, as the governed, from time immemorial, have petitioned their governors. But one day we abandoned our suit for petty damages, and instituted a suit for the recovery of our entire human heritage of freedom; and by basing our claim on the fundamental principles of the brotherhood of man and the sovereignty of the masses, we assumed championship of the oppressed against their oppressors, wherever found. . . . The American confession of faith, therefore, is a recital of the doctrines of liberty and equality.[19]

It is true that the sober findings of science and scholarship since 1776 have shaken the foundations of the natural-rights philosophy on which the Declaration was based, but the aspiration to realize the dream it held forth has nevertheless continued as strong as ever. As President Truman put it in his State of the Union message in January 1950, "At every point in our history, these ideals have served to correct our failures and shortcomings, to spur us on to greater efforts, and to keep clearly before us the primary purpose of our existence as a nation. . . . These principles give meaning to all that we do." [20]

V

Thus two basic sets of ideas or ideals, the one stemming from the Christian religion and the other from the Declaration of Independence, have sustained and refreshed the reform impulse. But great national crises, though less constant in effect, have also played a role. One may sympathize with Benjamin Franklin's view that there never was a good war or a bad peace and still recognize that the Revolutionary War—thanks partly to the lapse of British control—brought about such human gains in various states as a more democratic redistribution of land, the separation of church and state, the abrogation of primogeniture and entail and the first restraints on slavery and the slave trade. In like fashion the Civil War wrote into the Constitution the greatest of all American reforms, the total abolition of slavery. This showing, of course, can in no sense justify the spiritual and material costs of war. Probably most of these advances would have come sooner or later in any event, and the Civil War, moreover, actually set back such burgeoning reforms as temperance, women's rights and international peace. Besides, the moral letdown following an armed conflict often militates against social progress, as notably in the 1920's.[21] Yet war, within such limits, has actually contributed to human betterment.

The peacetime crises known as depressions have

exerted a more positive influence. In periods of general social dislocation, injustices long endured become intolerable, and men in their despair may even seek a passport to Utopia. The hard times following the Panic of 1837, for example, hurried many states into abolishing lotteries and imprisonment for debt, helped remove the restrictions on wives as to property rights, and generated forty or more short-lived collectivist communities. Similarly, the economic slump dating from 1873 speeded the movement for railroad regulation and for 'cheap money,' raised the Knights of Labor to national importance, and begot the Socialist Labor party as well as Henry George's panacea of the single tax. One need only recall the Great Depression of 1929, however, to realize to what extent a general economic collapse accelerates reform. It may appear unfortunate that so much of our social thinking has been done in abnormal times, but often the mind functions most clearly when action is imperative.

VI

Finally, it should be noted that the rhythm of reform has differed in different parts of the country; not all parts have advanced at the same speed or at the same time. In a nation nearly as large as Europe and almost as diversified as to local circumstances and interests, this is hardly surprising.

More than any other section, however, the South has resisted innovation. As slavery tightened its hold on the region and dimmed the ideals of the Revolutionary era, the people came to fear reform in general through fear of reform in particular—that one which would destroy the rock on which their society rested. Hence they derided as 'glittering generalities' the "self-evident" truths proclaimed by their own Jefferson in 1776, defended slavery as the most Christian of institutions, and erected an intellectual dike against 'subversive' Northern 'isms.' [22] Since the Civil War this conservative tradition has been sustained by the persisting race problem, the drain of potential dissidents into other parts of the country and the lack of material means to carry through reforms dependent on public funds. Hence the South, despite some signs to the contrary, continues to lag behind the procession of states.

It is more difficult to assess the reform roles of the two geographic sections lying north of the Mason and Dixon Line. Indeed, it is hardly worth trying, since between East and West there was a constant shuttling and sharing of experience. Despite a common impression that the West has always acted first, one need only recall that antislavery scored its initial victories on the Atlantic Seaboard before there was an established West, and that Congress, without consulting the people concerned, extended the blessings of freedom to the settlements in the territory north of the Ohio.

A truer view suggests that each region led in the reforms dictated by its local conditions or needs. For example, the agricultural West, as the years went on, championed a progressively liberal public-land policy and currency reform and initiated government control of grain elevators and railroads. It also embarked first upon woman suffrage, perhaps because the undersupply of women in the newly settled parts of the country spurred the men to vie for their favor, whereas in the older East men preferred to treat women as their 'superiors' rather than their equals. The East, on the other hand, focused on curing the evils created or intensified by its more complex industrial society: poverty, illiteracy, woman and child labor, low wages and bad factory conditions. In matters of common concern, however, like (white) manhood suffrage and 'trust busting,' the two sections acted almost simultaneously.

VII

This freedom of the various states to deal with their own problems in their own way has been a consequence of the American federal system. The Constitutional Convention of 1787 considered a consolidated type of government, but wisely settled upon the plan of limited national authority. Nothing could have proved a greater lubricant of social change. Federalism, as James Bryce remarked in *The American Commonwealth*, has allowed the people "to try experiments in legislation and administration which could not be safely made in a large centralized country," and this has enabled the whole group of states to "profit by the experience of a law or a method which has worked well or ill in the State that has tried it." [23]

Almost any successful reform would illustrate the point. Negro emancipation is not the best example because, though the Northeastern states pioneered the innovation, similar action by the other Northern states had in nearly every instance been assured by Congressional legislation eliminating slavery while they were territories. In the case of manhood suffrage, however, the principle had unrestricted play. The ballot, which was limited at the time of the adoption of the Constitution to property holders and taxpayers, was steadily liberalized state by state until at the time of the Civil War any white male citizen could vote. In like manner the states cut paths for each other in regard to public education, the regulation of the liquor traffic, the curbing of corporations, labor legislation and an endless number of other matters.

At certain points, however, federal action has supplemented state action, and this tendency increased as the country aged. The motive has been either to universalize a social change already well tested locally, or to protect progressive commonwealths against the harmful effects of inferior standards in other states, or to help poorer states carry the financial burden of reforms they could not otherwise afford. Sometimes the federal intervention has even involved altering the Constitution. Thus the three Civil War amendments conferred freedom and its attendant rights on the Negro in all the states, and the Nineteenth Amendment similarly extended the suffrage to women in all the states.

But experience with the prohibition amendment shows that action from above may overreach itself. This episode is a puzzling one. Not only was national prohibition preceded by a hundred years of local experimentation, but at the time of its adoption two thirds of the people—and over 95 per cent of the land area—had banned the liquor traffic in one way or another, and the amendment was ratified by ten more states than were required, just two short of the entire forty-eight. Yet it was repealed with equal alacrity less than fourteen years later. Perhaps the reason was that it had to breast the abnormal conditions created by the moral slump following World War I, when the law-abiding easily became law-breaking and the government itself was half-hearted about enforcement—a period, moreover, that was climaxed by the onset of the Great Depression. Besides, the prohibition amendment diverged from all others in seeking to police private and personal habits.

In a different way the amendments to guarantee civil and political equality to the Negro did not work as expected. In this instance, however, they were not repealed, and by remaining in the Constitution they are serving in our own day as a lever to secure the rights so long and wrongfully withheld.

VIII

For the most part, however, the general government has furthered reform by exercising powers already to be found in the Constitution. The first notable moves occurred when industrialization changed the face of the country and overran political subdivisions. The Interstate Commerce Act of 1887 and the Sherman Antitrust Law of 1890 came after efforts by individual states to solve these problems had failed. In the case of trusts, for example, the stubbornness of three states in chartering monopolies, which under the Constitution could do business also in all the other commonwealths, had confounded the attempts at local regulation. Stronger action by Congress along these lines followed in later years, together with a growing body of legislation to improve the economic position of wage earners, farmers and other groups. The constitutional basis for such measures was generally the interstate-commerce clause, which

attained horizons of meaning undreamed of in simpler times. Thus Congress's prohibition of child labor
in 1938, supplementing state measures, took the form
of banning from interstate shipment goods manufactured by companies employing children under sixteen
years of age or, in hazardous occupations, under
eighteen.[24]

Congress has also used its revenue power to abet
reform. The Constitution all along had authorized
the lawmaking branch to lay taxes to provide for "the
general welfare," but not till the twentieth century,
and particularly after the income-tax amendment, did
the government take multiple action along these lines.
On the one hand, it has levied taxes on incomes, inheritances and corporate earnings so graduated as to
bear most heavily upon the higher amounts and thus
promote a redistribution of wealth.[25] On the other
hand, it has devoted national funds to assisting or
bribing states to be more progressive. During the
Great Depression it exceeded even these bounds and
spent millions to provide the jobless with food and
work.

The system of subsidies to states affords perhaps the
most striking evidence of federal leadership in reform.
Though the precedents go back to the early land
grants for schools and colleges, the passage of years
has gradually broadened the program, added the feature of national standards which the recipients must

adopt, and in most instances has come to include reciprocal contributions from the states themselves.[26] The New Deal greatly stepped up this reform strategy, offering grants-in-aid and low-interest loans to states and municipalities not only for the older purposes, but also for such things as slum clearance, housing projects, old-age assistance and the public ownership of power plants. There can be no doubt as to who occupies the driver's seat because, if the national conditions are not agreed to, the funds are withheld.

Thus, as time has gone on, the balance in the federal system has shifted more and more toward the general government in the sphere of reform, as in so many others. Has this change gone so far as to deprive the states of their function as laboratories of social innovation? Interestingly enough, the present division of the Supreme Court between so-called conservative and liberal wings turns in considerable degree on this point. In principle both groups lean toward reform objectives, but the one wishes to preserve the traditional freedom of the states to make their own decisions, including the right to be wrong, while the other inclines to impose on them its own notions of expediency or wisdom.[27]

The advantages of federal intervention and leadership have already been noted, and certainly the expansion of national power on which it rests springs naturally from modern conditions. The critics, however,

stress the tendency of centralized direction and bu-
reaucratic control to sap local initiative and variety
to the nation's loss.[28] That this point has not yet
been reached is indicated by Nebraska's adoption of
a unicameral legislature in the 1930's and Georgia's
recent granting of the suffrage to eighteen-year-olds.
Nevertheless the need somehow to combine the bene-
fits of local creativeness and federal interposition,
without the drawbacks of either, is one of the crucial
challenges to the American public today. It is an
aspect of our national evolution which demands the
most thoughtful and continuous study.

THE REFORM IMPULSE
IN ACTION

2

THE REFORM IMPULSE
IN ACTION

"The history of reform," observes Emerson, "is always identical, it is the comparison of the idea with the fact." And that idea, as he says elsewhere, "is the conviction that there is an infinite worthiness in man, which will appear at the call of worth, and that all particular reforms are the removing of some impediment." [1] This faith in mere humanity derived its spiritual strength, as we have seen, from what forward-looking men regarded as both divine and natural law. But how was the idea to be put into effect, the impediment removed? At this point the friends of reform have usually divided. All might agree on the need of a social change and yet differ bitterly, even irreconcilably, over how to accomplish it. It should not be surprising that isms breed schisms considering the type of rebellious mentality upon which such movements draw.

I

Abolitionism affords an especially striking instance. Not only was it the greatest blow ever directed against human injustice in America, but it exhibited in sharp relief the conflicting attitudes of men seeking with equal earnestness the same goal. These attitudes sometimes overlapped, and they were not always consistently maintained. Nevertheless they illuminate the mental and temperamental differences that generally enter into the work of reform.²

One antislavery school consisted of men like Emerson and William Ellery Channing, who believed that all reform must begin with the individual, that you must remake souls before you remake institutions. They agreed with Pestalozzi that "the amelioration of outward circumstances will be the effect but can never be the means of mental and moral improvement." "It is better to work on institutions by the sun than by the wind," said Emerson, who scourged the "narrow, self-pleasing, conceited men" who mixed the "fire of moral sentiment with personal and party heats" and "measureless exaggerations." ³ "I know it is said," wrote Channing,

that nothing can be done but by excitement and vehemence; that the zeal which dares every thing is the only power to oppose long-rooted abuses. But it is not true that God has committed the great work of reforming the world to passion. Love is a minister of good only when it gives energy to the intellect, and allies itself with wisdom. . . . We ought to think much more of walking in the right path than of reaching our end. We should desire virtue more than success.

And he held as "immovably true" that, "if a good work cannot be carried on by the calm, self-controlled, benevolent spirit of Christianity, then the time for doing it has not yet come." [4]

Henry Thoreau, Emerson's neighbor and disciple, pushed this doctrine of inner regeneration still farther —to the point of passive resistance. He maintained that the lone man, once imbued with the idea, should not wait for others to see the light, but should act at once in his own sovereign capacity. "Must the citizen ever for a moment, or in the least degree, resign his conscience to the legislator?" he cried. ". . . It is not desirable to cultivate a respect for the law, so much as for the right." When Emerson found Thoreau in Concord jail for refusing to pay a tax toward the support of what abolitionists regarded as a proslavery war on Mexico, the older man is said to have asked, "Henry, why are you here?" and Henry to have replied, "Waldo, why are you not here?" In the famous essay on "Civil Disobedience," which grew out of his detention, Thoreau advised "those who call themselves Abolitionists" to cease their silly antics and "at once effectually withdraw their support, both in person and property, from the government." With "God on their side" they already were a majority.[5] But Thoreau's view had more influence on modern India than on his countrymen, and he himself as a supreme individualist did not join the only organization of the time that espoused like views.[6]

These high-minded New Englanders, in fact,

counted for little as compared with the apostles of "excitement and vehemence" whom they decried. When William Lloyd Garrison launched his paper *The Liberator*, he proclaimed,

I do not wish to think, or speak, or write, with moderation. No! no! Tell a man whose house is on fire to give a moderate alarm; tell him to moderately rescue his wife from the hands of the ravisher; . . . but urge me not to use moderation in a cause like the present. I am in earnest—I will not equivocate—I will not excuse—I will not retreat a single inch —AND I WILL BE HEARD.[7]

And Garrison was as good as his word. He left no stone unturned to arouse a mass demand for immediate and total emancipation. He beat his breast; he spoke and wrote; he defied mobs; he formed organizations; he pronounced the Constitution in Isaiah's words "a covenant with death and an agreement with hell," publicly burning it on one occasion; and he even advocated the North's secession from the South to remove the stain of complicity.

Garrison's immediatism, though closing many minds, blasted others open.[8] Himself a man of humble origin, deserted in infancy by a drunken father, he was soon joined in his crusade by the wellborn Boston lawyer and Harvard graduate, Wendell Phillips, who was prompted by seeing Garrison assaulted by a Boston mob. Phillips's subsequent career goes far toward justifying Dostoevski's observation that "an

aristocrat is irresistible when he goes in for democracy." He became antislavery's greatest orator, with
an impact on his audiences that made a Virginia editor
call him "an infernal machine set to music." [9]

In an address many years afterward at Harvard,
Phillips eloquently vindicated the Garrisonian type
of propagandist.

> Agitation [he said] is an old word with a new meaning.
> Sir Robert Peel, the first English leader who felt himself its
> tool, defined it to be "marshalling the conscience of a nation
> to mould its laws." . . . The agitator must stand outside of
> organizations, with no bread to earn, no candidate to elect,
> no party to save, no object but truth—to tear a question
> open and riddle it with light.[10]

In this spirit of dedication Phillips repudiated political
parties, because they valued votes over principles; and
he abandoned his legal practice rather than swear to
uphold a Constitution which condoned slavery. Like
Garrison, he wouldn't even vote, though both men,
of course, hoped to persuade the less pure of heart to
cast their ballots on the side of the angels.[11]

II

The sentiment these passionate men helped arouse
nursed into being still another antislavery group, one
which resorted to clandestine and lawless methods on
behalf of the oppressed race. Holding that the Fugitive Slave Act "set at naught the best principles of

the Constitution and the very laws of God," they patiently organized to subvert it. The Underground Railroad, however, is a special episode in the history of American reform since, except for some of the patriotic groups at the time of the Revolution, it is the single instance of an extensive secret movement to advance human rights by illegal means. The obscure men and women involved, law-abiding in their ordinary life, speeded the Negroes toward Canada by night and kept them in hiding by day. The system in time extended through fourteen Northern states and territories, with established routes for the refugees to follow. It is estimated that 75,000 slaves by this means stole their way to freedom.[12]

The Underground Railroad was a form of direct action which reached a tragic climax in John Brown's desperate attempt to raise a servile insurrection. The New England-born Brown was the type of uncompromising moralist that exists, potentially at least, on the edges of every turbulent reform movement. A lineal descendant of a passenger on the *Mayflower*, with two grandfathers who had fought in the Revolution, he had Hebraism in his marrow, emotional intensity in his blood. "He looked a Puritan of the Puritans, forceful, concentrated, and self-contained," Julia Ward Howe wrote in retrospect.[13] He may have had still another incalculable strain in his make-up, for both his mother and grandmother had died insane,

and an aunt and five cousins suffered the same afflic-
tion.

Working at first on the Underground Railroad in
Pennsylvania, he resolved to do the Lord's will more
effectively. In 'bleeding Kansas' he and four of his
sons massacred five pro-Southern settlers one night to
atone for the deaths of an equal number of antislavery men. Then, after a few years, he conceived
of a yet bolder stroke. With a band of eighteen followers he seized the federal arsenal at Harpers Ferry
in October 1859 to obtain weapons for arming the
Southern slaves against their masters. The little force
was quickly overpowered, and Brown was tried and
hanged. The nobility of his bearing after his capture
impressed all who saw him. Even the Virginia governor, Henry A. Wise, testified, "They are mistaken
who take Brown to be a madman. . . . He is a man
of clear head, of courage, . . . and he inspired me
with great trust in his integrity . . . ." [14] The antislavery cause had gained a martyr, but at the cost of
convincing Southerners that the North was seething
with violent designs against their cherished institution.

III

John Brown's raid was Garrison's dogma of immediatism carried to its logical conclusion. By rejecting
constitutional means of reform the Garrisonians

opened the door for lawless and irresponsible methods. The great majority of antislavery men, however,
while sharing Garrison's moral indignation against
slavery, advocated gradualism. Led by men like James
G. Birney, John Greenleaf Whittier and the Tappan
brothers, they insisted upon observing accepted democratic procedures within the limits fixed by the Constitution. They held to the Anglo-American principle
of reform by consent and parliamentary processes.[15]

At first they tried to infiltrate the old parties, and
when the results proved disappointing, many of them
turned to the third-party device, founding the Liberty party in 1839 and a series of successors until the
Republican party emerged in 1854. These parties demanded that the federal government use its authority
to blot out slavery in the territories and the District
of Columbia, and in most instances urged also the
repeal of slave-catching legislation. This resort to
politics helped create a breach in antislavery ranks,
with the Garrisonians retaining their hold on the
American Anti-Slavery Society and the political
abolitionists seceding to form a new one.

The greatest of all the gradualists was Abraham
Lincoln, an antislavery Whig who remained in his
party till a year or so after the Republican party was
formed. His statement that "A house divided against
itself cannot stand" might appear to indicate otherwise, but he was then speaking in a philosophical vein,

not as a political actionist.[16] The acid test came when as President he was confronted with Southern secession. To the anger and dismay of antislavery radicals, he scrupulously subordinated his personal convictions to his sworn duty to "preserve, protect and defend the Constitution," a course which endangered his leadership of the Northern masses. In his famous letter to Horace Greeley in 1862 he quietly affirmed, "If I could save the Union without freeing any slave, I would do it; and if I could save it by freeing all the slaves, I would do it; and if I could save it by freeing some and leaving others alone, I would also do that." [17]

Within this conception of policy he brought about abolition in the federal territories and the District of Columbia, offered financial aid for gradual emancipation in the four loyal slave states and, when at last convinced it was a "necessary war measure," he proclaimed the freedom of all Negroes in those parts of the South which failed to lay down arms within a hundred days. Universal liberation was achieved only by the Thirteenth Amendment at the war's close.

IV

Though gradualism thus came to express the dominant antislavery temper, it does not follow that the Northern conscience would have been aroused to this pitch except for the nongradualists. As a young man, Lincoln in 1837 had joined a fellow member of the

Illinois legislature in declaring that, while slavery was "founded on both injustice and bad policy," he believed "the promulgation of abolition doctrines tends rather to increase than abate its evils." [18] Contrast this with his more considered view as President, a year and a few months after the Emancipation Proclamation: "I have been only an instrument. The logic and moral power of Garrison, and the antislavery people of the country and the army, have done all." [19] In the interval he had come to understand that many ingredients, palatable and unpalatable, must enter into the successful brewing of a reform.

With equal insight he told Wendell Phillips in 1863 that the pioneer in a movement for social change is generally not the best person to carry it through. "It looks," he said, "as if the first reformer of a thing has to meet such a hard opposition and gets so battered and bespattered that afterwards, when people find they have to accept this reform, they will accept it more easily from any other man." [20] Phillips, for his part, though he had once castigated Lincoln as "the Slave-Hound of Illinois," paid him at last this grudging tribute:

No matter that, unable to lead and form the nation, he was contented to be only its representative and mouthpiece; no matter that, with prejudices hanging about him, he groped his way very slowly and sometimes reluctantly forward: let us remember how patient he was of contradiction, . . . how willing, like Lord Bacon, "to light his torch at every man's candle." With the least possible personal hatred; with too little sectional bitterness, . . . he welcomed light more than most men, was more honest than his fellows, and with a truth to his convictions such as few politicians achieve. . . . Coming time will put him in that galaxy of Americans which makes our history the day-star of the nations . . . .[21]

Lincoln, as a gradualist, could hardly be expected to approve of John Brown's rash exploit. Yet even on this he spoke with sympathy and understanding. In his Cooper Institute speech shortly after Brown's hanging, he observed,

This affair, in its philosophy, corresponds with the many attempts, related in history, at the assassination of kings and emperors. An enthusiast broods over the oppression of a people till he fancies himself commissioned by Heaven to liberate them. He ventures the attempt, which ends in little else than his own execution. Orsini's attempt on Louis Napoleon, and John Brown's attempt at Harper's Ferry, were, in their philosophy, precisely the same.[22]

Other Northerners, however, were swept off their feet by the foolhardy deed. Phillips cried, "Could we have asked for a nobler representative of the Christian North putting forth her foot on the accursed system of slavery?" and declared, "John Brown has twice as much right to hang Governor Wise, as Governor Wise has to hang him." Emerson, abjuring his insistence on individual regeneration and moral suasion, proclaimed that Brown had made "the gallows glorious like the cross," while Thoreau, the doctrinaire nonresistant, called the conviction a judgment not on the man, who was "an angel of light," but upon all America.[23] Emerson had evidently forgotten his earlier blast against fanatics: "They bite us, and we run mad also." [24]

V

This, indeed, was the verdict of the Southern people, who saw in the Harpers Ferry attack simply the final madness climaxing abolitionist ravings over thirty years. Back in 1835 the Bostonian William Ellery Channing had warned that the Northern propaganda was engendering in the South "bitter passions and a fierce fanaticism, which have shut every ear and every heart against its arguments and persuasions." [25] The youthful Lincoln, as has been seen, implied pretty much the same thing, and evidence of the Southern reaction rapidly mounted. The Georgia legislature posted $5000 for Garrison's arrest and conviction, a North Carolina grand jury indicted him *in absentia*, a Richmond mob burned him in effigy, and unofficial committees in many places offered rewards for apprehending him or anyone circulating his paper. Similar treatment was meted out to other Northern 'incendiaries.' The South also tightened its laws against the discussion of slavery, thus withholding the means of bringing about reform from within.

Yet the relation of cause and effect can easily be overstated. The initial reason for restricting freedom of speech and print was not the Northern propaganda, but Nat Turner's slave revolt in 1831 at Southampton, Virginia, which sent shivers of alarm down every slaveholder's spine.[26] Nor is it true that all Southerners were repelled by the Northern agitation. Individuals bravely continued to speak out against slavery in spite of the general attitude, while among the country's outstanding abolitionists were James G. Birney and the Grimké sisters, all of Southern aristocratic background, though they had to leave Dixie to carry on their work. Similarly the North Carolinian Hinton R. Helper had to flee the South after publishing his famous indictment of slavery: *The Impending Crisis of the South: How to Meet It* (New York, 1857), an attack on the system from the standpoint of the nonslaveholding whites.

There is, moreover, little evidence to support the opinion, often expressed then and since, that the South would have given up the institution of its own accord if it had not been baited and angered by Northern meddling. As a Southern historian of our own day has put it, "Although the abolition movement was followed by a decline of antislavery sentiment in the South, it must be remembered that in all the long years before that movement began no part of the South had made substantial progress toward

ending slavery. . . . Southern liberalism had not
ended slavery in any state." [27] To this it may properly
be added that, with servile labor in these later years
representing a capital investment of a billion or more
dollars, the possessing class could hardly be expected
to cut the ground from under its own feet.

The Civil War was America's greatest failure to
attain a social reform peaceably. It is sometimes asked
whether this catastrophe was avoidable, whether the
liberation of the Negro was worth the awful price.
But the question, however fruitful of idle speculation,
is meaningless historically.[28] If other men, godlike in
wisdom and operating in a political vacuum, had been
spokesmen for the two sides, the outcome no doubt
would have been different. But the inescapable facts
of history rendered this impossible. In the situation
that existed, abolitionism was as essential an ingredi-
ent as was slavery itself, and no amount of wishful
thinking by 'revisionist' historians can change this
fact.

Men took their stand, as they always do, for a complex of reasons—logical, psychological and traditional
—some of which they understood and some they did
not; they were prisoners of their time and place. As
Henry Ward Beecher remarked, Garrison "did not
create the anti-slavery spirit of the North: he was
simply the offspring of it." [29] That spirit reflected the
convictions of a people who, with no economic stake

of their own in slavery, fortified their social outlook from the New Testament, the Preamble of the Declaration of Independence and their daily practice of human equality. Moreover, they acted in harmony with an awakening world conscience. Not only had servile labor been recently outlawed in Mexico and the English, Danish and French colonies, but the Netherlands, Russia and Brazil were about to take similar action. Humanly speaking, the American abolitionists could not have done other than they did.

VI

Though the freeing of the slaves involved the biggest confiscation of private property in American history, the measure was in no sense a blow at the basic concept of private property. This would seem sufficiently clear from the fact that the party which carried it through became the greatest champion of property rights the United States has ever known; but it should also be noted that Lincoln himself, if events had not intervened, intended to cushion the shock of emancipation by compensating the owners, as was done in the case of the District of Columbia and as he offered to do in the border slave states. This program was poles apart from that of extremists who held that the Negro should be compensated rather than his oppressor, yet even such men had no wish to disturb the fundamentals of capitalism. In essence, the liberation of the black race purged the South of its last elements of feudalism and thus extended and strengthened the capitalist system.

This basic assumption as to the limits of reform is further underscored by the bootless efforts in the pre-Civil War period to transcend these bounds. Among the social innovators of the time were some who went off in little bands to live together and share all property and labor, hoping thus to light the way for the unregenerate world. "Communities were established where everything was to be common but common-sense," as James Russell Lowell put it.[30] The inspiration or initiative in nearly every instance came from Europe, where sensitive minds were reacting against the materialism and misery attending the Industrial Revolution, and the abundance of cheap land in America invited the attempts.

The first series of communities originated with the Scotsman Robert Owen; the second, with disciples of the Frenchman Fourier; and the third and last, with still another Frenchman, Cabet. These capsule ventures in socialism, though providing a colorful footnote in the annals of American reform, did not attract a total of over three or four thousand persons, and hardly any of the colonies lasted longer than a few years. Most reformers of the time were, as we have seen, both less ambitious and more successful: they strove simply to make the capitalist order more humane and more democratic.

Since the main stream of reform flowed between such well-defined banks, it is not surprising that the financial support as well as the leadership in these movements emanated generally from members of the middle class. Their benevolent intentions were not arrested by fears that the underpinnings of society would be ripped away. Though the bulk of the money came from small donors, the rich also helped. The New York businessman Arthur Tappan, for example, gave generously to such objects as antivice, antitobacco, antislavery, temperance and Sabbath observance; and the Boston merchant Charles F. Hovey willed $40,000 for "the promotion of the Anti-Slavery Cause and other reforms" (women's rights, peace, temperance and free trade).[31]

This attachment of the well-to-do to unpopular causes has, moreover, continued in later times, as a multitude of instances would show. It is perhaps sufficient to recall that, with possibly a single exception, the wealthiest presidential candidates since the Civil War have headed small protest parties: Peter Cooper, the Greenback nominee in 1876, and Henry A. Wallace, the ex-New Dealer who in 1948 was inveigled into running for the Communist-dominated Progressive party.

VII

All this sheds an interesting light on the much-discussed economic interpretation of history. Do materialistic motives always determine the course of human events? Is the pocket nerve the sole governing force in society? If so, the majority of reforms could never have been achieved, and men of substance would not have lent them aid and comfort. Obviously, history cannot be reduced to a simple conflict between rich and poor, between the haves and have-nots, for too many other factors enter in.[32]

For one thing, men with economic security often feel freer to give rein to their humanitarian sympathies, and are financially in a better position to do so, than the less secure; under American conditions they are carrying on the tradition of *noblesse oblige*. For another thing, the possessing class is not in fact the solid phalanx that the Marxists have represented. Business and agriculture, for example, often have conflicting interests, and it is not unusual for business itself to divide into contending factions.

Moreover, the average citizen, even when believing himself to think in economic terms, frequently does not understand where his selfish advantage lies, or else doesn't know how to balance a short-term benefit against a long-term advantage. Most historians, for example, agree that the Midwestern farmers who clung so long to the Republican party and its fetish of the protective tariff were standing in their own light, and that similarly Bryan's followers in the free-silver campaign were acting against their real self-interest. In like manner the Southern poor whites before the Civil War were upholding an oligarchy which was oppressing them almost as much as the Negroes. In other words, the economic motive, even when appearing to operate, may do so in such a confused and disconcerting way as to rob the term of genuine meaning.

On the other hand, it would be folly to maintain that altruism has supplied the only incentive to political and social action. Yet when Calvin Coolidge uttered his famous sentiment, "The business of America is business," he justly added, "The chief ideal of the American people is idealism." [33] The point is that there is a tender-hearted as well as a tough-minded streak in the national character; and in the struggle for highly controversial reforms the two strains have had to be blended in correct proportions to spell success.

In the case of antislavery, for instance, sympathy for the downtrodden Negro dominated the early stages of the movement, but the majority of Northerners remained indifferent until a series of events in the 1850's—the Kansas-Nebraska Act, the Dred Scott decision and Buchanan's veto of the homestead bill—

convinced them that the South was plotting to keep them and their children out of the beckoning federal territories. Lincoln's platform of 1860 skillfully played on both strings. Thus the self-interest of the white man gave the necessary lift to the emotions created by pity for the slave.

The drive for colonial dependencies and spheres of influence in the late nineteenth century exhibits this formula unhappily in the reverse. The design of powerful business interests to acquire new sources of raw materials and to promote overseas investments and trade won little popular response until it was pictured as a means of carrying Christianity to the benighted heathen and, more broadly, of shouldering what Kipling called "the white man's burden." Who could resist such an unselfish appeal? Protests that this course violated the historic American doctrine of the consent of the governed, and that "no nation can long endure half republic and half empire," went unheeded.[34] But if imperialism was a case of sugar-coating the pill, the sweetness disappeared when experience revealed that the financial disadvantages outweighed the advantages for both the business community and the government. Then the values in the equation changed, and in the 1930's the United States with general approval swiftly renounced the program. American idealism may be fooled some of the time but, in Lincoln's phrase, not all of the time.

The ethical aim of reform—the persistent "comparison of the idea with the fact"—has time and again enlisted literary figures in the struggle. Their perceptive minds react readily to human injustice, and their pens, tipped with moral sensitivity, often carry conviction where the professional agitator batters against stone walls. They also reach readers who would be bored by political or sociological disquisitions. Abolitionism had its poet laureate in John Greenleaf Whittier, who "made his song a sword for truth," and its fictional champion in Harriet Beecher Stowe, whom President Lincoln is reported to have called "the little woman who wrote the book that made this great war!" By the same token, *Ten Nights in a Bar-room* (1854) was the *Uncle Tom's Cabin* of the temperance movement, and, to mention only a few other examples, the years since then have brought forth such conscience-stirring books as Edward Bellamy's *Looking Backward* (1888), Jacob A. Riis's *How the Other Half Lives* (1890), Upton Sinclair's *The Jungle* (1906) and John Steinbeck's *The Grapes of Wrath* (1939).[35] It is a significant commentary on the spiritual appeal of reform that no comparable voices have ever been raised on the other side.

VIII

With rare exceptions the purpose of reformers is to induce favorable action by some governmental authority: the legislature in the case of a state, Congress in the case of the nation. In order to kindle the necessary outside support the humanitarians in the first half of the nineteenth century set the example of creating a host of nation-wide voluntary bodies, each with its special palliative or panacea. As described by a contemporary, the first step was to choose an "imposing" designation for the organization; the second, to obtain "a list of respectable names" as "members and patrons"; the next, to hire "a secretary and an adequate corps of assistants"; then "a band of popular lecturers must be commissioned, and sent forth as agents on the wide public" and the press be "put in operation"; finally, "subsidiary societies" must be "multiplied over the length and breadth of the land." [36] So thoroughly did these crusaders work out the pattern of reform organization and propaganda a hundred years ago that later generations have found little to add beyond taking advantage of new communication devices such as the movies and the radio.

The American two-party system, however, has posed constant difficulties for reformers. The reasons for this twofold political alignment need not be considered here, though it is worth noting that it is historically a characteristic of English-speaking peoples as contrasted with other nations. The point is that this duality seldom engenders the polarization of convictions which might theoretically be expected:

'me-tooism' is no mere modern phenomenon. The established parties wish to stay established, and to do so they are forced to seek a formula which will bring the many different regions and interests together in an acceptable program, as well as to unite the liberals and conservatives within their own ranks. They strive for the common denominator, to please as many as possible and offend as few as possible, with the result that compromise and evasion become the rule. As an old-line politician is quoted as saying, "Let me make the deals and I care not who makes the ideals."

Whatever objections may exist to this practice, the major parties have, with the tragic exception of 1860, always succeeded in inducing the public to accept the outcome of elections, and even in that lone instance they had staved off the sectional crisis for forty years. Walter Lippmann, indeed, has extolled this habit of opportunism as the "noblest achievement of democracy," for it means that "the solidarity of the people in a free society is stronger than their division into parties" and "that their capacity to find common ground is stronger than all the many interests that divide them." He holds that "a nation, divided irreconcilably on 'principle,' each party believing it is pure white and the other pitch black, cannot govern itself." [37]

This may be conceded as true in an absolute but not in a relative sense. A more venturesome attitude by the two parties toward pathbreaking social and economic ideas in line with the American reform tradition would clearly not endanger democracy. On the contrary, it would buttress it by giving the voters a clearer alternative at the polls, by enhancing party responsibility and by tending to keep the government more nearly abreast new needs. Reformers have always rejoiced when a Jackson or Wilson or Roosevelt defied political orthodoxy, but such occasions have been few, occurring only when abuses had accumulated to a point where they could no longer be ignored.

IX

To counter the customary practice of the old parties, reform groups have from time to time launched their own parties. The earliest of these date from before the Civil War, but their real flowering came later. The 1872 election was the first with as many as three minor parties; the 1900 campaign had nine; and 1948 saw seven.

Broadly speaking, these organizations have been of four types. One series comprised what may be called single-track parties, of which the Prohibition party, founded in 1869, alone still survives. Other specimens in the later nineteenth century were the Greenback party (1876–1884); the Anti-Monopoly party (1884); the Equal Rights party (1884–1888), which ran a woman for President to dramatize the fact that women could not vote; and the United Christian party (1900), which aspired to put the name of Christ in the United States Constitution. With the exception of the Prohibitionists none of this breed outlasted more than a few elections, and no new ones of note have arisen in the twentieth century.

The second sort consisted of parties urging the demands of occupational interests, notably the farmers and the wage earners, the two great groups disadvantaged by the rise of Big Business. Working within the reform tradition, they sought governmental intervention to assure them some of the personal dignity and economic independence which their forebears had enjoyed. The agrarian parties—the Populists in 1892 are the best example—proposed such steps as free silver, the government ownership of railroads and the popular election of Senators. The Labor Reform party (1872) and the Union Labor party (1888), for their part, asked for measures like shorter hours, factory legislation and currency reform.

Such efforts, however, collided on the one hand with the Western farmers' sentimental attachment to the Republican party and on the other with the hostility of key labor leaders to hazardous political adventures. Moreover, the best hope for success lay in uniting the two occupational interests, but attempts to do so never got far. The farmers, rooted in the

soil, distrusted the landless wage earner, and being
obliged by the nature of their task to toil when necessary from dawn to dusk, they could no more sympathize with the desire of urban workers for shorter
hours than the latter could with the farmers' desire for
higher crop prices. The Farmer-Labor party of 1920
and La Follette's Progressive party in 1924 tried to
bridge the gap, but neither outlived the single election.[38]

The third variety of these movements aimed at dis-
placing the capitalist system. The first Marxist party
appeared in the campaign of 1892, and by 1900 there
were two in the field. Unlike the other instances, the
socialist doctrine was imported from Europe and ap-
pealed largely to naturalized citizens still thinking in
European terms. At its peak, in 1920, the Socialist
party, the stronger of the two, mustered 920,000
votes, most of them undoubtedly of a protest rather
than an ideological character; and both groups have
continued to function to the present time.[39] Mean-
while, under the spell of the Bolshevik revolution in
Russia, a leftist offshoot in 1919 formed the American
Communist (originally the Workers) party, whose
leaders have come into repeated conflict with the
courts on charges of conspiratorial methods, allegiance
to a foreign power and an intent to overturn the government by force. The Communist vote, however, has
never exceeded 103,000 (in the depression election

of 1932), and in the last two campaigns—1944 and 1948—the party has not even ventured to run presidential candidates under its own label.[40]

The final kind of minor party is represented by temporary splits from one or the other of the established groups. Since the Civil War this has happened about every twenty years, the outstanding cases being the Liberal Republican party of 1872 (which joined with the Democrats in that election); the Gold Democrats and Silver Republicans in the 1896 contest; Theodore Roosevelt's Progressive party in 1912; and the Dixiecrats in 1948.[41] The cause in each instance was a clash of principles or personalities or both. It should be noted, however, that the splinter party is not necessarily animated by reform ideals, as witness the Dixiecrats who left the Democratic fold over the question of Negro rights.

As for the three other types of parties, their idealism cannot in most cases be questioned, but their reform effectiveness can. Historians have stressed the utility of these movements in ventilating unpopular issues and in arousing sufficient voter support to cause the old parties to espouse the proposals. Though the educational function undoubtedly exists, it seems small as compared with the widespread and unflagging efforts of private nonpolitical bodies to promote the same objects. Thus, though minor parties have agitated such causes as woman suffrage, farm relief and

factory legislation, the real work of mobilizing opinion has fallen to powerful nonpartisan groups whose
spiritual lineage goes back to antislavery times.

Nor is it clear that these parties have done much
to impose reform views on the regular parties. Only
twice in modern times have they marshaled sufficient
strength to break into the electoral college. True, on
the first occasion, in 1892, the Populist victories
frightened the Democrats into adopting a free-silver
plank in the 1896 campaign; but the disastrous outcome of this action, besides failing to accomplish the
supposed reform, steeled old-line politicians against
similar third-party threats in later years. On the second occasion, in 1924, when La Follette polled some
electoral votes (and 16.5 per cent of the popular ballots), the effect on the older organizations was negligible.[42] The real aim of minor parties, of course, is to
become major parties, but this has never happened
since the Republicans, starting in 1854 as a third
party, became in their first presidential election the
second party. One wonders if the marvel can ever be
repeated in view of the difficulties of tradition, organization, finance and legal impediments, all of which
are infinitely greater than they were a century ago.

To some extent, moreover, minor parties have done
positive harm to reform. By their very nature they
tend to drain strength from the more progressive of
the old parties, since they recruit voters who, come

hell or high water, want the whole loaf instead of only part. In a close race they may even defeat the more liberal party and thereby bring on worse evils. A notable instance—to go back to antislavery days—is the election of 1844 when the Liberty party won enough votes in New York state to assure James K. Polk a plurality over Henry Clay and thus give the presidency to the more hated foe, who in due course instigated the Mexican War and added more potential slave territory to the Union. In the 1948 contest the Wallace Progressives could only have hoped to undercut the Democrats and so bring into power the more conservative of the major parties. And according to the ordinary operation of American politics they should have succeeded; but in this miracle election the Democratic nominee triumphed without the support of either New York, where the Wallace vote threw the state to Dewey, or of the Solid South.[43]

X

Because of the shortcomings of the third-party method, reformers in recent years have turned increasingly to the pressure-group device. This was a technique borrowed from the enemy, for Big Business had long demonstrated its efficacy in obtaining tariff legislation and other special favors. It involves systematic lobbying, high-powered propaganda to convert the public, campaigns to get out the vote and contributions to the war chests of existing parties. Though reform organizations may be hampered by smaller funds, they possess equal zeal, and the method enables them to take their demands direct to legislative bodies and administrative officers, to bore from within the major parties, and while assisting friends, to threaten enemies with political extinction. Besides, whenever a need is felt with sufficient intensity, an organization can be created and set functioning in a matter of days or weeks. In the national scene the current activity of organized labor in regard to the Taft-Hartley Law illustrates the pressure-group tactic.

Today the number of these groups for all purposes in Washington has come to compose a veritable third house of Congress. In 1942 a total of 628 maintained offices there, a majority of them for what their sponsors regarded as reform objects. Four years later Congress took official cognizance of the situation by requiring the agents to register, with a statement of their purposes, sources of income and expenditures.[44] By 1948 more than 1100 were listed, outnumbering the elected members of Congress almost three to one. In this manner the reform spirit has developed a concentrated energy and effectiveness undreamed of by Garrison and Phillips in the more primitive days of the Republic.

Though the 1946 registration law has deprived the

system of its more obvious abuses, the thoughtful may still wonder whether it conduces to the greatest good of the greatest number. There is not the direct responsibility to the voters as in the case of political parties, and, moreover, some causes succeed better than others merely because of stronger financial backing. These are weighty objections, yet it should be remembered that the reform movement, even in its simpler stages, displayed similar features. The principal difference today is that, in a country highly organized in every other field, reform itself has had to take on a highly organized character. In the battle of the giants, with all points of view represented, including the opposition to reform, we citizens of a free society may expect truth and enlightenment to continue to emerge and the nation be correspondingly the gainer.

THE REVOLT AGAINST REVOLT

THE REVOLT AGAINST REVOLT

"The two omnipresent parties of History, the party of the Past and the party of the Future, divide society to-day as of old," observes Emerson.[1] It is, of course, the ever-shifting Present over which the battle is constantly being waged. The reasons animating the forward-looking party have perhaps been sufficiently examined. It remains to consider the opposition to reform.

I

The most durable barrier to change, it need hardly be said, is human inertia, a trait which man appears to have derived from his animal ancestors. An Englishman, visiting the United States in the 1830's, at a time he might have noted signs to the contrary, said on this point,

certain doctrines and opinions . . . have descended like heirlooms from generation to generation . . . . The sons succeed to these opinions of their father, precisely as they do to his silver salvers, or gold-headed cane; and thus do certain dogmas, political and religious, gradually acquire a sort of proscriptive authority and continue to be handed down, unsubjected to the test of philosophical examination.[2]

And the aging James Russell Lowell, once himself a flaming reformer, agreed. "Things in possession have a very firm grip," he remarked in lecturing on "Democracy" in 1884. "One of the strongest cements of society is the conviction of mankind that the state of things into which they are born is a part of the order of the universe, as natural, let us say, as that the sun should go round the earth." [3] In this last allusion Lowell was obviously poking fun at the adversaries he had encountered some forty years before, but this in no wise detracts from the essential truth of his observation.

The reformer, in other words, is a disturber of the peace. He trespasses on forbidden ground and commits assault and battery on human complacency. His offense, moreover, is compounded by other considerations valued in varying degrees by the society he assails. These may be summarized as a reasoned disinclination to tamper with a political and social framework that has stood the test of time (lest the cure be worse than the disease); a belief that a minor unsettlement will beget a major one (hence a step in the right direction would be a step in the left direction); an unwillingness to forfeit an economic advantage (why should superior enterprise be penalized?); a psychopathic horror of change under any circumstances (it is always better to let well enough alone); a craving for the social approbation which inheres in supporting the *status quo;* and, finally, a fatalistic despair of remedying conditions in any event (so why try?).

Not of least importance is the fact that many are turned against proposed social cures by distrust or disapproval of the self-appointed doctors and surgeons. The reformer is apt to be self-righteous, untidy in dress, truculent, humorless, with a single-track mind and an almost ostentatious liking for the hair shirt and martyrdom: he makes virtue repulsive. Besides, he is frequently so indiscriminate in his choice of causes, taking on all comers, that the underdog appears to have him on a leash. In addition, he is often a failure at his own business, and though a strident lover of mankind, may neglect his family and shirk his neighborhood obligations. Horace Greeley, out of fullness of knowledge, mentioned particularly the sort who know "the Social edifice is wrong end up from the fact that they are so near the bottom of it," and those who hope by remaking the world to achieve "wealth without industry, enjoyment without obedience, respect without virtue."[4] These hangers-on compose what Theodore Roosevelt called "the lunatic fringe" and James Russell Lowell "the whistle and trailing fuse of the shell."[5]

Unfortunately, history never succeeds in making clear to posterity that the shock troops of reform are almost necessarily captained by the headlong and the ungenteel—men of explosive temperament and rude manners. This failure of the historian arises from the fact that, when the battle is won, the innovation ac-

quires such an aura of respectability that later generations cannot believe it could ever have been seriously
opposed. A conservative has been defined as a man
who has grown fond of the order which liberals have
forced on him. Even ultraconservatives come to re-
vere revolutions of the past without altering their
undying resistance to the mildest reforms of the present. "Your fathers killed the prophets and ye build
monuments to them," Jesus chided the Scribes and
the Pharisees. And so Boston, which once persecuted
Anne Hutchinson, Wendell Phillips and William
Lloyd Garrison, has erected statues to them, and on
their pedestals they wear so dignified a mien that
James Russell Lowell wrote of one of the sculptures:

> There's Garrison, his features very
> Benign for an incendiary.[6]

Little wonder, then, that conservatives, never understanding how social progress has taken place in the
past, continue to be repelled by the irritating qualities
of reformers.

II

Some of the rooted objections to reform—as well
as the flaws of some reformers—are well illustrated by
Frank R. Stockton's tale of the medieval town of
Rondaine.[7] Probably this half-forgotten author merely
intended to write another of those engaging fantasies

which once endeared him to the youthful of all ages, but the story's broader implications are inescapable. It begins when the youthful heroine Arla, listening in bed one morning to the multitudinous clocks that studded the steeples and towers and streets, suddenly realized that they never struck at the same time. How then, she wondered, could the people know when Christmas, then approaching, would actually begin? Hardly able to wait till her own tiny bedside clock bade her get up, she sallied forth with it to apprise the townsfolk of the situation.

"Good morning, sir," she curtsied to the sacristan of a church, "you should know that your clock is eleven minutes too fast. Won't you please set it straight?" "How good of you, little Arla," he growled, "but while you're about it, aren't there other things you would like to set straight? How about moving those pillars so as to make it easier for people to come in? Or turning over those great beams in the roof to give a fresher appearance to the ceiling?"

Arla, rebuffed but not disheartened, hurried to the town square, where a stone figure sounded the hours with a hammer. "If you please, sir," she said to the bent caretaker, "your clock is a little off. The stone man sometimes strikes seven minutes late." "Child," he replied weightily, "for one hundred and fifty-seven years the thunder and lightning have roared and flashed around that clock; kings and queens have come to the throne and passed away. Yet through all this time that stone man has stood there doing his duty. Of all the things that were able to lift an arm, he alone is left. And now you, a child of thirteen, would ask me to change what has not been changed for a century and a half and seven years!"

Arla, nonplused, trudged on to the tiny shop of a cobbler with a clock above the door. "Your clock," she informed him gently, "is the most irregular in all Rondaine. Sometimes it strikes as much as twenty-five minutes late, sometimes not at all." "Ah," returned the cobbler, "it is clear you have never been a shoemaker, or you would know that customers get angry when their boots aren't ready on time. So when I am behindhand, I set back the hands and the people gladly wait until I have finished. Sometimes I have to stop the clock altogether." "Then you will not make it go right?" she asked. "That I will do with all cheerfulness," he answered in true Emersonian spirit, "as soon as I can make myself go right. The most important thing should always be done first."

Arla next plodded on to the covered bridge, which had a clock at either end. "Do you know, sir," she said to the bridgekeeper, "that the one at this side is two minutes faster than the other?" "You are as wrong as wrong can be," snapped the venerable man. "Though I be too deaf to hear them strike, I have often looked at this one and then, afflicted as I am with rheumatism, have hobbled to the other end of the bridge and have always found the clock there exactly like it."

Now increasingly discouraged, Arla wended her way along a dusty road to a great country estate on the outskirts. There the attendant in charge of the clock listened with mounting horror to her request. "The altering of the time of day," he declared solemnly, "is a matter not to be considered lightly. If you set back the hands even as little as ten minutes, you add that much to the time that has gone. No human being has the right to add anything to the past. On the other hand," he continued, "if you move the hands forward, you take that much away from the future. These are matters with which mortal kind should never trifle."

Though Arla sensed something wrong with this reasoning, she could not quite put her finger on it, and she decided to appeal to a little old lady whose clock was the slowest in all Rondaine. But the goodwife bristled at the thought. "Never in my life," she cried, "have I been so spoken to! My grandfather lived in this house; that clock was good enough for him! My father and mother lived in this house; it was good enough for them! I have always lived in this house; it is good enough for me! Sooner than raise my hand against the clock of my ancestors I would cut it off!" "But," ventured Arla timidly, "I don't doubt your clock is a good one. I only meant that you could make it better." The little old lady, moved by the tears in Arla's eyes, answered more kindly, "Child, you do not know what you are saying, and I forgive you. But remember this: never ask persons as old as I to alter the principles which have always governed their ways."

Determined upon one final effort, Arla proceeded to the great town hall, where an iron donkey chimed the hours by kicking a bell. The custodian listened patiently, then looked grave. "The donkey," he explained, "is a very complicated mechanism, depending on a great many wheels and cogs and springs, and these are subject to expansion and contraction due to heat and cold. There is no way to make the donkey keep better time unless the citizens should buy new works for the clock, and that's not likely since all but yourself seem perfectly satisfied."

"I suppose that's so," Arla sighed, "but what a pity that all the clocks of Rondaine should be wrong!" "How do you know they are?" he inquired. "Because none of them agrees with my own little clock." She proudly handed it to him, and he took it away for a moment. Returning, he shook his head. "I have compared your timepiece with my sundial," he announced, "and find it ten minutes slow." "What!" she exclaimed in dismay and then, more slowly, "I'll stop comparing other clocks with mine. If the people don't want theirs to keep good time, there is nothing I can do about it." "Especially," chuckled the custodian, "since you can't be sure your own is right."

These objections to reform have a familiar modern ring. In today's terms, the burghers were 'rugged individualists' united against any move to tinker with the existing order. The sacristan deemed Arla a revolutionary who, if gaining her present object, would seek to uproot other cherished institutions. The attendant of the stone man rested his case on immutable custom. The cobbler found justification in economic self-interest. The bridgetender flatly denied that anything was wrong. The caretaker of the country estate sought refuge in sounding abstractions. The little old lady took offense at the insult to her forebears. And the technically minded keeper of the iron donkey raised innumerable mechanical objections. Though everyone had his special reasons, the group occupied common ground in condemning the reform as an infringement on personal liberty and a ruthless attempt at regimentation.

Nor was Arla herself without fault. Eager to achieve a civic improvement, she had not critically examined her own proposal, and when she was shown its defect, self-pride kept her from correcting it by harmonizing her clock with the sundial. Considering the simple times in which she lived, she can more easily be excused for not forming an organization, putting committees to work and circumventing the opposition by building a backfire of community opinion.

III

As Lowell reminds us in his essay on "Democracy," "Not a change for the better in our human housekeeping has ever taken place that wise and good men have not opposed it . . . ." [8] American history abounds with examples, but a few will suffice to point the moral.

The Tories at the time of the American Revolution, as is well known, embraced many persons of wealth and position, including important landholders and merchants as well as prominent lawyers, clergymen and college graduates. John Adams—and no one should have known better—estimated that a third of the people were against independence, and another third indifferent or neutral. The Tories contended that with patience the troubles could still be solved peaceably without casting off British rule and that the commercial disadvantages of separation outweighed any possible gains. In any case, they maintained, the colonists would be licked, with "the blood of thousands bedewing the ground, and the whole wealth of the continent, the whole labor of a century, vanished in the air," and that, even if they succeeded, the enfeebled country would quickly fall prey to foreign aggression. As one of the group wrote, "In whatever light we consider this truly Utopian project, . . . the more impracticable, absurd, and ridiculous it appears"; and, as another said, "A set of men whom nobody knows . . . are attempting to hurry you into a scene of anarchy; their scheme of Independency is visionary; they know not themselves what they mean by it." [9] If one may judge by some of the reactionary attitudes of the Daughters of the American Revolution in our own day, it would appear that they have forgotten from which side of the great struggle they trace descent.

The proponents of (white) manhood suffrage met with like resistance. On every hand people of substance and education pictured the fatal effects that would ensue. In Massachusetts, Daniel Webster and Justice Story joined with the venerable John Adams in combating it. In Virginia, James Madison, Chief Justice Marshall and John Randolph—men who had often been pitted against each other in the past—made common cause against it. Nor can their reasons be lightly dismissed. They warned against the dangers of rule by "King Numbers," that is, by the "ring-streaked and speckled population of our large towns and cities, comprising . . . every kindred and tongue," and insisted that only property holders had the sense of responsibility needed for wielding political power wisely. In the words of the eminent New York jurist Chancellor Kent, "Universal suffrage jeopardizes property and puts it into the power of the poor and the profligate to control the affluent." "I hope, sir," he implored, that "we shall not carry desolation through all the departments of the fabric erected by our fathers." [10] In Rhode Island the resistance was so strong as to require a civil war to bring victory. Although the opposition everywhere eventually failed, the arguments were to be dusted off fifty years later and used, with appropriate modifications, against woman suffrage.

The case against the emancipation of black Americans was no less redoubtable, enlisting as it did the support of practically all the statesmen, jurists, churchmen and college professors in the South as well as some in the North. [11] They pointed out that four of the first five Presidents, not to mention several later ones, had held slaves and, more important, that the institution enjoyed Biblical sanction. Furthermore, it was vindicated by the latest findings of science, for ethnologists asserted that the Negro's racial characteristics stamped him as an inferior order of human being. In any event, freedom would precipitate a bloody race conflict which could end only in exterminating the Africans.

On the positive side, slavery was justified as a beneficent system assuring the Negroes paternalistic care, regular employment and, in their declining years, the equivalent of an old-age pension. "Sickness need not frighten nor old age awe," as the *Charleston Courier*, June 27, 1855, declared. What a happy contrast to the inhumanity visited by Northern industrialists on their white wage-slaves "tantalized with the name of freedom, to which their condition gives the lie." These degraded toilers received starvation pay, constantly trembled for their jobs, and in the end were cast aside like rusty tools. But the institution's greatest value lay in its contribution to social and intellectual achievement. All history from Greek times attested this fact, since human bondage alone made possible that necessary division of labor upon which all cultural advance rests. As Senator James H. Hammond of South Carolina expounded this thesis,

In all social systems there must be a class . . . to perform the drudgery of life. . . . Such a class you must have or you would not have that other class which leads progress, civilization, and refinement. It constitutes the very mud-sill of society and of political government; and you might as well attempt to build a house in the air, as to build either the one or the other, except on this mud-sill.[12]

So fixed were these convictions that they had to be blown to bits by four years of warfare, and to this day the doctrine of 'white supremacy' lingers in some Southern minds.

The contemporaneous demand for free public

schools encountered obstacles almost as stubborn. Senator Hammond's mud-sill argument as to the blessings of slavery had a curious counterpart in the remonstrances against universal education. As a Philadelphia newspaper editor put it, "The peasant must labor during those hours of the day which his wealthy neighbor can give to abstract culture of his mind; otherwise, the earth would not yield enough for the subsistence of all"; nor could the mechanic "abandon the operations of his trade, for general studies; if he should, most of the conveniences of life . . . would be wanting; languor, decay, poverty, discontent would soon be visible among all classes." As though these reasons were not enough, the writer further denounced the proposal as "virtually Agrarianism. It would be a compulsory application of the means of the richer for the direct use of the poorer classes; and so far an arbitrary division of property among them." Rather than suffer such an act of tyranny, it "would be resisted at the point of the bayonet," declared foes of the reform in the Rhode Island legislature.[13]

Other objections were no less plausible. The providing of education without charge would cause the children of the poor to grow up lazy. It would be government interference in the relations of parent and child. It would violate the vested rights of the private and parochial schools. By an unexpected twist in the argument it was at the same time contended

there was priestcraft in the scheme, since the establishment of a state school would open the way for the
establishment of a state church. Finally, the enormous
cost would saddle the states with chronic deficits. For-
tunately, however, other views prevailed, and the
United States was thus enabled to make one of its
greatest contributions to world civilization.

IV

The hostility to economic reforms is perhaps more
familiar, but one instance is worth recalling because
its merit too is now universally acknowledged. In
1894 Congress adopted an income tax, mild enough
by current standards, since it exempted all personal
earnings below $4000 and assessed higher ones a mere
2 per cent. The country was in the trough of a depression, and the proponents of the law had demanded
that a part of the tax burden be adjusted in accord-
ance with the principle of ability to pay.

In 1895 the question of its constitutionality came
before the Supreme Court. The distinguished lawyer,
Joseph H. Choate, besides urging legal objections to
the measure, branded it as "communistic" and "socialistic." "I have thought," he said,

that one of the fundamental objects of all civilized governments was the preservation of the rights of private property
. . . that it was the very keystone of the arch upon which
all civilized government rests, and that this once abandoned,
everything was at stake and in danger.

Calling Congress's action part of a "communistic march," he declared, "I do not believe that any member of this Court has ever sat or ever will sit to hear and decide a case the consequences of which will be so far-reaching as this."

The Court a quarter of a century before had unanimously upheld an earlier income-tax law, but now a majority of one sided with Choate. Justice Field in his concurring opinion solemnly warned, "The present assault upon capital is but the beginning. It will be but a stepping stone to others, larger and more sweeping, till our political contests will become a war of the poor against the rich; a war constantly growing in intensity and bitterness." A sigh of relief swept through the business world. The *New York Tribune* cried, "The fury of ignorant class hatred, which has sufficed to overthrow absolute power in other lands . . . has dashed itself in vain against the Constitution of the United States, fortified by the institutions which a free people have established for the defence of their rights." And the *New York Sun* exclaimed, "The wave of socialistic revolution has gone far, but it breaks at the foot of the ultimate bulwark set up for the protection of our liberties. Five to four the Court stands like a rock." [14] The federal taxation of incomes came to a halt until the country, at the suggestion of a stalwart Republican President, amended the Constitution in 1913.

The tremors of alarm evoked by proposed innovations, the frightened outcries of socialism and radicalism, persist even in the twentieth century. When Roosevelt was in office, the conservative press flayed him as the "Great Leveler," shuddered at the "Reign of Terror," and, in the words of the *Philadelphia Record*, declared he had given "more encouragement to state socialism and centralization of government than all that frothy demagogues have accomplished in a quarter of a century of agitation of the muddy waters of discontent." [15] When he decided on a third term, a New York editor asserted,

The menace of the Roosevelt campaign does not lie in the third-term tradition, but in the state of mind that could desire four years more of Roosevelt in the White House, four years more of personal government, four years more of Presidential lawlessness, four years more of autocratic rule, four years more of executive contempt for Congress, courts and Constitution, four years more of centralization, four years more of wanton extravagance, four years more of denunciation and demagogy—in the state of mind that wants the new national aims, that wants a Federal interference with every form of human industry and activity, that wants the states stripped of their powers, that wants the minority and bureaucracy substituted for the Bill of Rights. . . . The danger does not lie in popular indifference to the third-term tradition, but in popular indifference to the fundamental principles of liberty upon which the Republic was established.[16]

Lest the unwary reader shout too hasty an amen, he should know that all these charges were leveled, not against Franklin Roosevelt, but against his elder kinsman 'Teddy.'

v

The attempt to influence opinion and settle intricate public problems by opprobrious epithets ill becomes the greatest and best educated democracy in the world. There is nothing so potent in popular discussion as catchwords and scratch words—words that win favor for a cause with a telling phrase and those that excite dread of the alternative with a distorted image. Such tactics doubtless arise from an over-eagerness to win adherents, and it is well known that reason and logic make fewer converts in a year than a well-chosen slogan can in a week. Sloganeering is a sort of magnifying glass for focusing attention, but like a magnifying glass it produces heat as well as light. Leaders of thought betray the public interest by resorting to symbols of emotion and prejudice. Would it were feasible to have a pure-food law that applied to adulterated language!

The practice, however, is an old one. It began in the Revolutionary period when George III was gibbeted as a 'tyrant,' though he had little or nothing to do with the colonists' grievances. In the 1790's the Federalists smeared Jefferson's followers as 'democrats,' a term then with bad associations because of the French Revolution, while Jefferson returned the compliment with aspersions like "monarchist" and "monocrat." The two sides in the sectional controversy indulged in similar exchanges. Though Garrison mourned that the *Liberator's* "hard language" fell short of "the enormous guilt of the slave system" and considered the English vocabulary "lamentably weak and deficient in regard to this matter," he could nevertheless pillory Southern Congressmen as "desperadoes. . . . We would sooner trust the honor of the country in the hands of the inmates of our penitentiaries and prisons. . . . We do not acknowledge them to be within the pale of Christianity, of republicanism, of humanity." And the Southerners retorted by denouncing the "foul slander" of "the fire-brands of discord and destruction," whom none other than the president of South Carolina College described as "atheists, socialists, communists, red republicans, jacobins." [17]

With shifting times and issues this battle of labels has continued to the present day. Currently the Republicans, long out of power, have been seeking a scratch word to counter the catchwords 'New Deal' and 'Fair Deal.' In the 1930's 'bureaucracy' and 'regimentation' were tried and found wanting, yet as late as 1944 Joseph W. Martin, Jr., Republican leader of the House, was still execrating the drift toward "a regimented nation, with absolute control vested in a power-mad group of bureaucrats and social planners." [18] More recently, party leaders have experimented with the terms 'collectivism,' 'statism' and 'welfare state,' and the policy declaration of the Republican National Committee in February 1950 defined the issue before the country as "liberty against socialism." [19] Such expressions have been designed to frighten the public with reminders of what has happened to the Russian people and to picture England's democratic socialism as a despotism in the making. In the latter case, though, it is never mentioned that Mr. Churchill's Conservative opposition stands to the left of even the Fair Dealers in the United States.

Granted the ever-present need of a strong political minority to keep the majority party on its toes, do these slur words make for popular clarification or for intellectual smog? The effort to besmirch the term 'welfare state' seems particularly reprehensible. Ex-President Hoover in a speech in August 1949, on his seventy-fifth birthday, called it "a disguise for the totalitarian state" and declared that the nation was already "on the last mile to collectivism." The following November, Governor Thomas E. Dewey, Republican standard-bearer in the last two presidential elections, took his turn at blasting the "ever-growing, nobody-can-feed-you-but-us philosophy of the welfare state," and other party stalwarts joined in. Three months later, however, in calmer mood, Governor Dewey confessed in an address at Princeton, "The man who first used the phrase against the present Government did his cause no good, to put it mildly," and went on, "Anyone who thinks that an attack on the fundamental idea of security and welfare is appealing to the people generally is living in the Middle Ages." [20]

Indeed, one of the avowed aims of the "more perfect union" consummated by the United States Constitution had been to "promote the general welfare," and the years that followed saw the governments of both states and nation increasingly alert to interpret the function in broadly human terms. The emancipation of the slaves was the act of a welfare state; the giving of free farms to the landless was another; public education still another. In Lincoln's view, "The legitimate object of government is to do for a community of people whatever they need to have done, but cannot do at all, or cannot so well do for themselves, in their separate and individual capacities." [21]

Faithful to this creed, the Republican party for many years sponsored legislation to police Big Business in the public interest, promote state universities, conserve natural resources and improve working conditions. Even after they lost control of the federal government, and notably since 1936, their platforms have asserted a growing responsibility of the nation for social welfare. The 1948 pronouncement cited in justification another statement of Lincoln's: " 'The

occasion is piled high with difficulty and we must rise
to the occasion. As our case is new, so we must think
anew and act anew.' " Then the platform continued:
"The tragic experience of Europe tells us that popular
government disappears when it is ineffective and no
longer can translate into action the aims and the as-
pirations of the people." [22]

I suggest that for responsible thinking in this criti-
cal period of our history the need is to appeal from
Philip drunk to Philip sober. No one, not even Mr.
Hoover, really believes that the basic idea of the welfare state is at stake; but questions of how and when
and where the concept should be applied are.[23] How
fast and far should we go? How much can we afford
without draining the financial sources of support? At
what point will the government's intervention begin
to sap individual initiative and independence? To
what degree are social services a function of the states
rather than of the general government, and to what
extent should private voluntary effort carry the burden? These are matters that require the most search-
ing and objective examination. They cannot be wisely
decided by verbal pyrotechnics that merely confuse
the issue.

The charge of 'socialism' is even more misleading,
and it has been repudiated by some Republican leaders. The term 'welfare state' may lack precise definition, but this is not so of 'socialism' which, even in

its milder versions, involves a very considerable state ownership or nationalizing of the machinery of production and distribution. No spokesman of the New Deal or Fair Deal has ever advanced such a program unless a regional development like the TVA be included, and that undertaking has come to enjoy the approval of both major parties. Again the critics merely contribute to mental obfuscation and so distract attention from the questions that might usefully be debated.

VI

Probably no terms, however, have ever been more badly mauled through the years than 'American' and 'Americanism.' To the historian these words denote the abiding effort to realize the goal of Jefferson's great Preamble and the social teachings of Christianity, but too frequently they have been stolen by bigoted enemies of these principles. The first political party to use the name "American party" was backed by a secret organization, the Order of the Star-Spangled Banner, which exacted of its members an oath to "vote only for native-born American citizens for all offices" and for "the exclusion of all foreigners and Roman Catholics in particular." The initiates were assured that they would thus "keep alive in their bosoms the memory, the maxims and the deathless example of our illustrious Washington." This was too much for even the proslavery Democrats, who in their 1856 platform flayed this "political crusade in the nineteenth century, and in the United States of America, against Catholic and foreign born" as violating the inherited "spirit of toleration and enlarged freedom." [24] Nevertheless these self-styled Americans mustered strength for a time in a surprising number of states.

In the late 1880's arose the American Protective Association, a secret order disseminating anti-Catholicism through its journal *The American Patriot* with the assistance of countless rabble-rousers. Enlisting a million or more members, it helped elect William McKinley governor of Ohio in 1893, but it also provoked a stinging rebuke from Theodore Roosevelt on "What Americanism Means" in the *Forum* the next year. On a different plane, but with a similar patrioteering purpose, the National Association of Manufacturers after World War I put forward what it called the "American Plan" of no trade-unions (or of company-dominated unions) to counter labor's own efforts to improve working conditions. At about the same time the Ku Klux Klan began its terroristic campaign for "100-per-cent Americanism," that is, "white, native, Protestant supremacy," denouncing with fine impartiality Catholics, Jews, Negroes, internationalists, pacifists, birth-control advocates and Darwinian evolutionists.

Presently the Moscow-minded Communists announced, "Communism is twentieth-century Americanism," and proclaimed their mission to "forward the democratic traditions of Jefferson, Paine, Lincoln and Frederick Douglass." [25] As World War II approached, pro-Nazi and anti-Semitic groups here and there coalesced under such names as the Ultra-Americans, the American Nationalist party, the American Destiny party, the American Patriots and the Crusaders for Americanism, while another isolationist organization, not intentionally allied with these stealthy bands, preached far and wide the gospel of "America First." [26]

In view of this dubious historical record, thoughtful citizens feel a natural distrust of an official body named the House Committee to Investigate Un-American Activities, in existence since 1938. What is the yardstick of 'un-Americanism,' and are politicians, aching for reëlection and artful at showmanship, the best judges to apply it? When J. Parnell Thomas, then chairman of the Committee, was invited to take part in a Brooklyn College radio program on "Who and What Is Un-American?" President Gideonse relates that that worthy objected "that it was indecent and shameful for a college to discuss such a subject, that words like American and un-American did not require definition because everyone knew what they meant, that we didn't have the right to discuss it." When informed that the Bill of Rights indicated otherwise, he replied "that he didn't care about the Bill of Rights." [27] Representative Thomas was later sent to prison for misspending government funds.

The continued existence of the Committee implies that the Department of Justice, the FBI and the courts have not done their duty, but if this is so, the remedy would appear to lie in invigorating those arms of the government. Since, however, the Committee shows no signs of retiring from the scene, elementary fairness requires that the persons accused be granted the customary Anglo-American safeguards of due process of law. But nothing in the Committee's record of character assassination and irresponsible publicity under cloak of Congressional immunity is reassuring as to this. 'Un-Americanism' has tended to coincide with views the members personally dislike; and what they dislike won them in 1942 the accolade of the Imperial Wizard of the Ku Klux Klan.

The Committee would not have fared well in Lilliput. As Lemuel Gulliver wrote of his visit to that land,

All Crimes against the State, are punished here with the utmost Severity; but if the Person accused make his Innocence plainly appear upon his Tryal, the Accuser is immediately put to an ignominious Death; and out of his Goods or Lands, the innocent Person is quadruply recompensed for the Loss of his Time, for the Danger he underwent, for the

Hardship of his Imprisonment, and for all the Charges he hath been at in making his Defence.[28]

VII

That the Committee has occasionally turned up evidences of Communism in government hardly justifies its witch-hunting procedures, for in the course of so doing it has not only blackened the reputation of innocent citizens, but it has intimidated many who in the American democratic tradition were merely urging reform by constitutional methods. It has, moreover, nourished a popular mood that has substituted hysteria for common sense. The story is told of the man who, being clubbed by a policeman, called out, "I'm not a Communist, I'm an anti-Communist," and the officer replied, "I don't care what kind of a Communist you are!" Whether this ever happened or not, the San Diego city council not long ago did actually negative a reference to the Four Freedoms in the inscription of a World War II memorial because, on the advice of a retired admiral, "Freedom from want is a Russian communistic slogan." A month later, though, the council, daunted by protests from the men who were to be honored, backtracked to the extent of allowing the veterans' groups to decide the matter for themselves.[29]

As Raymond B. Fosdick, former president of the Rockefeller Foundation, has written,

If you sign a petition to admit colored people to public housing developments, if you favor fair employment practices or are concerned about civil liberties, if you fight for the protection of the rights of the foreign born, if you oppose religious prejudice and Jim Crowism, if you sanction cultural exchange with foreign countries, if you align yourself with those who are working for more effective labor unions or more adequate medical care, if you take any point of view which involves the implementation of the Declaration of Independence that all men are created equal, you are apt to be suspected in some circles as a knowing participant in the Communist Front, or at the very least, as a witless dupe of Moscow's hypnotic influences.[30]

To the historian such fevers and fears evidence a sorry lack of faith in American ideals and in the capacity of free institutions to command the people's continuing confidence and allegiance. Communism is a world threat. It is a cruel hoax which has tricked or coerced millions of confused and hungry men into trading their hope of liberty for a police tyranny. In the United States, so far as it has won adherents and sympathizers, it is a foe of peaceful methods of reform; and as a political party obedient to a foreign power, it poses a problem without historical precedent. In fact, however, it has marshaled a negligible voting strength even in the depths of the Depression, and it has failed signally with the one class in the population whose unhappy plight might have caused them to listen: the Negroes.

In our detestation of Communism we must not,

however, do irreparable harm to our American heritage of freedom. Abhorring authoritarianism, we must
not substitute an authoritarianism of our own, match
repression with repression, and become like the thing
we loathe. Nothing would please Russia's rulers more
—if indeed it is not their deliberate purpose—than to
stampede us into actions that would appear to identify
America not with the forward-looking movements of
mankind, but with a bleak and frozen *status quo*.
That is the picture the Kremlin is trying to paint of
us, and that, unfortunately, is the picture some
thoughtless and panicky people in the United States
are unwittingly trying to help it paint.

This does not mean that we should not know our
enemies and be alert to their designs. We cannot do
this, however, if, as is sometimes proposed, we outlaw
the Communist party and render the plotters invisi-
ble. On the other hand, we cannot for a moment tol-
erate men of divided loyalties in positions of power,
especially in the so-called sensitive areas of the government such as the State Department and the Department of Defense. But this is a task requiring con-
summate judgment and skill, and if we are true to our
traditions, it must be discharged with due legal safeguards for the persons suspected. The federal administration has embarked upon such a program, and
every citizen should be on watch to see that the venture does not exceed its legitimate bounds. Certainly

the novel concept of 'guilt by association' is one
deeply disturbing to lovers of liberty.

VIII

The assault on the educational system as a nursery
of Communism and subversive doctrines is another
danger to democracy. It is an old American custom
to blame the schools and colleges for whatever goes
wrong, and no educator will deny that the system has
many shortcomings. But a purpose to destroy the
government has never been one of them. After all,
education is primarily an agency for transmitting
tested knowledge, and the classrooms are staffed with
men and women who represent a cross section of the
population. Nonetheless, after World War I there
was an epidemic of loyalty-oath laws which singled
out the teaching profession as their target; and since
World War II, despite the legislation already on the
statute books, a set of definitely anticommunist oaths
has been added. By June 1949, tests of this new kind
were prescribed for public-school teachers in twenty-
five states and for college and university instructors
in twenty states.[31] In some other places equivalent
regulations are administered by the governing boards
of institutions of higher learning without a law.

Now out of the more than a million Americans
engaged in teaching, perhaps a tiny fraction of 1 per
cent are believers in Communism, and scarcely any of

this handful would be detected or dislodged, because of the known Communist willingness to swear to lies. The more likely effect will be to strangle independence of mind on the part of teachers in general and thereby turn education into a species of thought control. As the United States Commissioner of Education has recently said,

Children are not sent to school to be indoctrinated with a closed system of philosophy or the political views of the teacher. . . . But in our efforts to avoid one danger, we must not embrace another. The present period of hysterical concern must not betray us into adopting measures of censorship and control which are the essence of the police state.[32]

If the public has any confidence at all in a profession which has always been outstanding for its loyalty, it will be content to let the members themselves expose any colleagues who abuse their trust. A basic criterion for teaching at every level is competence in the particular subject, and no instructor can qualify whose prior commitment to an ideology forbids the free pursuit of truth. Schools and colleges do not lack means of getting rid of such offenders. Therein lies the only rightful remedy.

There have been other times in American history when a bad state of nerves has tended to cripple democratic energies, and each time the patient has recovered. With Russian totalitarianism an indefinitely persisting menace to Western civilization, however, it behooves every citizen to be vigilant as never before. But intellectual delirium tremens is not the answer. Rather, let us put our faith in the historic principles that have raised the United States to its present position of moral leadership in the world.

From the beginning, American democracy has been a method of evolution, a developing conception of human worth springing from Christianity and the doctrine of the rights of man. With James Russell Lowell we have held, "There is only one thing better than tradition, and that is the original and eternal life out of which all tradition takes its rise." [33] Our national life has been healthy and virile because of the opportunity to criticize, protest and espouse unpopular causes. The reformer has always had his day in court, and if his case was good enough, he has won the verdict. We have striven to act in the spirit of Wendell Phillips when he said,

> Let us always remember that he does not really believe his own opinion who does not give free scope to his opponent. Persecution is really want of faith in our creed. . . . He who stifles free discussion, secretly doubts what he professes to believe is really true.[34]

We have never regarded democracy as a finished product but something to keep on building. In this sign we have grown great and strong. In the years ahead it may be the key to national survival.

COMMENTARY AND NOTES

COMMENTARY AND NOTES

The American as reformer is inescapably present in every extensive account of American history, for such has been the nature of the people who settled and built the Republic. Few historians if any, however, have specifically examined the general character and workings of the reform impulse. The present venture is an introduction to the subject which, it is hoped, will prompt others to prosecute more comprehensive inquiries. In a sense this book continues an interest in American national traits which found earlier expression in *New Viewpoints in American History* (New York, 1922), *Learning How to Behave, a Historical Study of American Etiquette Books* (New York, 1946) and *Paths to the Present* (New York, 1949).

For the opportunity of preparing the present essays I am grateful to the Haynes Foundation of Los Angeles and to President E. Wilson Lyon and his colleagues of Pomona College who provided me with a platform as well as a richly rewarding intellectual experience. In expanding the essays for publication I have had the benefit of suggestions from my wife Elizabeth Bancroft Schlesinger, Arthur M. Schlesinger, Jr., and my secretary Elizabeth F. Hoxie, to whom I am under further obligation for typing the manuscript and compiling the index. For the title of the third essay I am indebted to the subtitle of Peter Viereck's *Conservatism Revisited* (New York, 1949).

The reader may wish to pursue certain ramifications of the subject further. Leon Whipple, *The History of Civil Liberty in the United States* (New York, 1928), Gustavus Myers, *History of Bigotry in the United States* (New York, 1943), and Zechariah Chafee, Jr., *Free Speech in the United States* (Cambridge, 1941), which stresses the twentieth century, shed light on the difficulties confronting social innovators. Much information on the relation of religion to reform can be gleaned from W. W. Sweet, *The Story of Religion in America* (rev. ed., New York, 1939); R. B. Perry, *Puritanism and Democracy* (New York, 1944), a work of broader scope than the title indicates; and Alice F. Baldwin, *The New England Clergy and the American Revolution* (Durham, 1928). For more recent developments A. I. Abell, *The Urban Impact on American Protestantism, 1865–1900* (Cambridge, 1943), C. H. Hopkins, *The Rise of the Social Gospel in American Protestantism, 1865–1915* (New Haven, 1940), and H. F. May, *Protestant Churches and Industrial America* (New York, 1949), to 1895, should be consulted.

Among the few period studies dealing with reform movements collectively are J. F. Jameson, *The American Revolution Considered as a Social Movement* (Princeton, 1922), and Alice F. Tyler, *Freedom's Ferment* (Minneapolis, 1944), which describes the varied enthusiasms of the generation before the Civil War. Of particular undertakings there are many accounts, including K. H. Porter, *History of the Suffrage in the United States* (Chicago, 1918); Inez H. Irwin, *Angels and Amazons, a Hundred Years of American Women* (Garden City, 1933); F. R. Dulles, *Labor in America* (New York, 1949); J. H. Franklin, *From Slavery to Freedom* (New York, 1947), a history of the American Negro; Merle Curti, *Peace or War, the American Struggle, 1636–1936* (New York, 1936); R. A. Woods and A. J. Kennedy, *The Settlement Horizon* (New York, 1922); Blake McKelvey, *American Prisons* (Chicago, 1936), on penal reform; J. A. Krout, *The Origins of Prohibition* (New York, 1925); D. L. Colvin, *Prohibition in the United States* (New York, 1926); A. E. Bestor, Jr., *Backwoods Utopias, the Sectarian and Owenite Phases of Communitarian Socialism in America: 1663–1829* (Philadelphia, 1950); and W. A. Hinds, *American Communities and Co-operative Colonies* (rev. ed., Chicago, 1908). Abolitionism has received the lion's share of attention, the interest in the subject in recent years being shown by such studies as G. H. Barnes, *The Anti-Slavery Impulse, 1830–1844* (New York, 1933); W. S. Savage, *The Controversy over the Distribution of Abolition Literature, 1830–1860* (Washington, 1938); D. L. Dumond, *Anti-Slavery Origins of the Civil War in the United States* (Ann Arbor, 1939); A. Y. Lloyd, *The Slavery Controversy, 1831–1860* (Chapel Hill, 1939); Clement Eaton, *Freedom of Thought in the Old South* (Durham, 1940); Henrietta Buckmaster, *Let My People Go, the Story of the Underground Railroad and the Growth of the Abolition Movement* (New York, 1941); and R. B. Nye, *Fettered Freedom: Civil Liberties and the Slavery Controversy, 1830–1860* (East Lansing, 1949). In addition, nearly all the major reformers have had full-length biographies, some of which are cited in the notes that come later.

The function of minor parties as reform instruments is favorably portrayed in a group of recent works. W. B. Hesseltine, *The Rise and Fall of Third Parties* (Washington, 1948), is a short general sketch, while Nathan Fine, *Labor and Farmer Parties in the United States, 1828–1928* (New York, 1928), T. H. Greer, *American Social Reform Movements: Their Pattern since 1865* (New York, 1949), and M. S. Stedman, Jr., and Susan W. Stedman, *Discontent at the Polls, a Study of Farmer and Labor Parties, 1827–1948* (New York, 1950), treat the movements based upon occupational interests. S. J. Buck, *The Agrarian Crusade* (New Haven, 1920), and J. D. Hicks, *The Populist Revolt* (Minneapolis, 1931), provide additional information on farmers' parties, and C. McA. Destler, *American Radicalism, 1861–1901* (New London, 1946), is valuable for stressing the interplay of Eastern and local influences in Western reform movements. Morris Hillquit, *History of Socialism in the United States* (rev. ed., New York, 1910), and James Oneal and G. A. Werner, *American Communism* (rev. ed., New York, 1947), tell the story of the anticapitalist parties. For pressure groups, see Stuart Chase, *Democracy under Pressure* (New York, 1945); H. L. Childs, *Labor and Capital in National Politics* (Columbus, 1930), and Childs, ed., *Pressure Groups and Propaganda* (American Academy of Political and Social Science, *Annals*, CLXXIX, 1935); K. C. Crawford, *The Pressure Boys* (New York, 1939); and E. P. Herring, *Group Representation before Congress* (Baltimore, 1929).

The footnotes that follow include citations to other writings, as well as to some of those that have already been listed, in connection with particular topics.

I. THE HISTORICAL CLIMATE OF REFORM

1. "Man the Reformer," *Works* (Boston, 1883–1887), I, 217, 218, 220.

2. See A. M. Schlesinger, *Paths to the Present* (New York, 1949), 174–177, 181–183.

3. "The Fortune of the Republic" (1878), *Works*, XI, 410–411. For a similar analysis, see George Gibbs, *Memoirs of the Administrations of Washington and John Adams* (New York, 1846), I, 1.

4. *North America* (New York, 1862), 218. J. T. Adams amplifies this point in *The Epic of America* (Boston, 1931), 99–100.

5. "The Fortune of the Republic," *Works*, XI, 411.

6. The exact percentages were: upper class, 6; middle class, 88; and lower class, 6. W. A. Lydgate, *What Our People Think* (New York, 1944), 159–160.

7. *New York Times*, February 2, 1950; "Big Unions Turn to Capitalism," *United States News and World Report*, XXVIII, no. 13 (March 31, 1950), 41–43.

8. For an example of the latter attitude, see H. J. Laski, *The American Democracy* (New York, 1948), and for an American expression of a similar point of view, John Chamberlain, *Farewell to Reform* (New York, 1932).

9. As R. B. Nye says in *Fettered Freedom: Civil Liberties and the Slavery Controversy* (East Lansing, 1949), 251, the net effect of these and other infringements "was to gain for abolition

a body of supporters who thought less of the wrongs of the slave than of the rights of the white man. . . . The antislavery movement flourished under persecution."

10. "On Conciliation with the Colonies" (1775), *Speeches and Letters on American Affairs* (*Everyman's Library*, London, n.d.), 93.

11. Peter Oliver, Origin and Rise of the American Rebellion to 1776 (F. L. Gay Transcripts, Massachusetts Historical Society), 73. For fuller discussions, see Alice M. Baldwin, *The New England Clergy and the American Revolution* (Durham, 1928), and C. H. Van Tyne, *The Causes of the War of Independence* (Boston, 1922), chap. xiii.

12. Alcott applied the term specifically to the Reverend Samuel J. May who wrote and spoke for such reforms as Negro emancipation, women's rights, public education, temperance and universal peace. G. B. Emerson and others, *Memoir of Samuel Joseph May* (Boston, 1873), 232.

13. O. B. Frothingham, *Gerrit Smith* (New York, 1877), 62.

14. William Lloyd Garrison's angry epithet was "the black-hearted clergy." For an abolitionist bill of particulars, consult James G. Birney's *The American Churches, the Bulwarks of American Slavery. By an American* (rev. ed., Newburyport, 1842). W. W. Sweet, *The Story of Religions in America* (New York, 1930), 426–447, makes clear the nature of the internal problem for the churches.

15. Bryce observed in *The American Commonwealth* (2-vol. ed., London, 1888), II, 583, that religion and conscience were a "constantly active force" in America, "not indeed strong enough to avert many moral and political evils, yet at the worst times inspiring a minority with a courage and ardour by which moral and political evils have been held at bay, and in the long run generally overcome." Note also the Swedish sociologist Gunnar Myrdal's comment in *An American Dilemma* (New York, 1944), I, 10–12.

16. From John 10:10: "that they might have life, and that they might have it more abundantly."

17. Address at the Arlington National Cemetery, December 21, 1949, *New York Times*, December 22, 1949. A Gallup

poll a few years ago indicated that 94 per cent of the American people believe in God and only 3 per cent do not. *Public Opinion Quarterly*, VIII (1944), 580.

18. Zechariah Chafee, Jr., *Free Speech in the United States* (Cambridge, Mass., 1941), 410.

19. *They Who Knock at Our Gates* (Boston, 1914), 3–7.

20. Message of January 4, 1950, *Boston Herald*, January 5, 1950.

21. As President Wilson remarked presciently to Josephus Daniels when pondering intervention in World War I, "Every reform we have won soon will be lost if we go into this war. We have been making a fight on special privilege. . . . The people we have unhorsed will inevitably come into the control of the country for we shall be dependent upon the steel, oil and financial magnates. They will run the nation." R. S. Baker, *Woodrow Wilson, Life and Letters* (Garden City, 1927–1939), VI, 506 *n*.

22. In "dissecting this pretended maxim" (that all men are created equal) a Virginian stated, "Its truth is certainly very far from being self-evident, or rather its truth is self-evident to some, while its falsehood is self-evident to others, according to the side from which it is viewed." A. T. Bledsoe in E. N. Elliott, ed., *Cotton Is King, and Pro-Slavery Arguments* (Augusta, 1860), 320. For the South's rejection of Revolutionary liberalism, see Clement Eaton, *Freedom of Thought in the Old South* (Durham, 1940); W. S. Jenkins, *Pro-Slavery Thought in the Old South* (Chapel Hill, 1935); and J. S. Robert, *The Road from Monticello* (Durham, 1941). Eaton, whose chap. xii treats "The Intellectual Blockade" against the North, quotes the South Carolinian H. W. Ravenel (p. 330) as vaunting the South as "the breakwater which is to stay that furious tide of social and political heresies . . . . which are infecting the masses in Europe and the free states of the North."

23. Bryce further pointed out that the state constitutions, being more easy to amend than the Federal Constitution, have more nearly kept pace with the changing needs of society through conferring new functions on the state governments. *American Commonwealth*, I, 344–345, 506.

24. A law of 1916 based on the same principle had been annulled by the Supreme Court five to four in 1918, but the later one was unanimously sustained in 1941. C. B. Swisher, *American Constitutional Development* (Boston, 1943), 587–588, 966–967.

25. President Coolidge declared, "I do not believe that the Government should seek social legislation in the guise of taxation," but his Secretary of Commerce, Herbert Hoover, approved of "the present inheritance, income and excess profits taxes" as tending "to a better distribution of wealth." C. A. and William Beard, *The American Leviathan* (New York, 1930), 342. For a historical study of the taxing power "as a social force in democracy," see Sidney Ratner, *American Taxation* (New York, 1942).

26. This evolving program encountered constant opposition. As a Virginia Senator viewed the Morrill Act of 1862 (for subsidizing colleges devoted primarily to agriculture and the mechanic arts), it was "an unconstitutional robbery of the Treasury for the purpose of bribing the states." Beards, *American Leviathan*, 669. As if to answer this critic, the United States Supreme Court in 1923 upheld the federal-aid law then under attack, adding, "Nor does the statute require the States to do or yield anything. If Congress enacted it with the ulterior purpose of tempting them to yield, that purpose may be effectively frustrated by the simple expedient of not yielding." A. F. Macdonald, *Federal Aid* (New York, 1928), 258, a work which surveys the system historically.

27. See T. R. Powell, "Behind the Split in the Supreme Court," *New York Times Magazine*, October 9, 1949, 13 ff. Of course, this issue of judicial restraint versus 'judicial legislation' is an old one. For example, the *American Law Review*, criticizing the Court's adverse decision in 1895 on the income tax, asserted, "some of the judges of that court seem to have no adequate idea of the dividing line between judicial and legislative power, and seem to be incapable of restraining themselves to the mere office of a judge." Ratner, *American Taxation*, 214. In like spirit Justice Oliver Wendell Holmes later admonished his brethren: "Great constitutional provisions must be administered with caution . . . . and it must be remembered that legislatures are ulti-

mate guardians of the liberties and welfare of the people in quite as great degree as the courts." And again: "in dealing with state legislation upon matters of substantive law we should avoid with great caution attempts to substitute our judgment for that of the body whose business it is in the first place, with regard to questions of domestic policy that fairly are open to debate . . . ." Felix Frankfurter, ed., *Mr. Justice Holmes* (New York, 1931), 64–65.

28. As an editorial on "State Abdication" in the *Boston Herald*, December 31, 1949, argued in regard to federal subsidies, "There is no assurance that states will spend their money wisely or even as well as the federal government. But the state government is closer to the people; it can be better watched; its spending is more closely related to its taxing . . . . There is less chance under state spending that federal agencies will develop powerful lobbies and propaganda machines. . . . There is more likelihood that spending programs will be adapted to the states themselves, that Massachusetts will not be compelled to follow a line suitable for Kentucky or North Dakota."

II. THE REFORM IMPULSE IN ACTION

1. *Works* (Boston, 1883–1887), I, 237 ("Man the Reformer"), 258 ("Lecture on the Times").

2. One approach to the problem of slavery, that represented by the American Colonization Society, is omitted from the present discussion because it so quickly lost its character of a reform effort. Supported at first by such antislavery leaders as Garrison, Gerrit Smith, Theodore Weld and the Tappan brothers, these men turned against it as they came to believe that the transporting of freedmen to Liberia was actually strengthening the slavery system by ridding it of the more intelligent and discontented bondsmen. They were also made suspicious by the active participation of prominent slaveholders in the Society. As for the Negroes themselves, a meeting of three thousand in Philadelphia in 1817 denounced the deportation plan. Moreover, as Garrison pointed out in 1830, the Society in thirteen years had removed only thirteen hundred Negroes while the slave population had

increased by perhaps half a million. E. L. Fox, *The American Colonization Society, 1817–1840* (Baltimore, 1919); Lewis Tappan, *The Life of Arthur Tappan* (New York, 1870), 135; W. P. and F. J. Garrison, *William Lloyd Garrison* (New York, 1885–1889), I, 149.

3. *Works*, I, 241 ("Man the Reformer"), 263, 267 ("Lecture on the Times").

4. "Slavery" (1835), *Works* (Boston, 1882), 733–734. Nevertheless, elsewhere in this discussion (p. 725), he declared that forcible emancipation "would be better than everlasting bondage; but the responsibility of so conferring it is one that none of us are anxious to assume."

5. *Cape Cod and Miscellanies* (Boston, 1929), 358, 369.

6. This was the New England Non-Resistance Society, which managed to keep going from 1838 to 1849. Founded by leftists in the peace movement, it pledged its members (who probably never exceeded two hundred) to obey their consciences rather than the government, but to submit meekly to any penalties that might result. The pledge singled out military service and the holding of offices that entailed the inflicting of imprisonment or death. "As for achievement," says Merle Curti in *The American Peace Crusade* (Durham, 1929), 86, "it was almost a case of beating bare fists against granite." Adin Ballou, one of the group, wrote an elaborate defense of the doctrine: *Christian Non-Resistance in All Its Important Bearings* (Philadelphia, 1846), based upon the Biblical text: "I say unto you, resist not evil." Tolstoy acknowledged the influence of this treatise on his pacifist views. Garrison was a member, but not always a consistent exemplar of the tenets. The fullest account is Curti, "Non-Resistance in New England," *New England Quarterly*, II (1929), 34–57.

7. Issue of January 1, 1831, quoted in Garrisons, *Garrison*, I, 225.

8. In antislavery circles the term 'immediatism' was sometimes used to mean merely the immediate beginning of steps toward the eventual extinction of slavery, but the more common meaning was the one given in the present discussion.

9. Ralph Korngold, *Two Friends of Man* (Boston, 1950), 179,

a work which admiringly treats the interrelated lives of Garrison and Phillips.

10. "The Scholar in a Republic" (1881), *Speeches, Lectures, and Letters* (2d series, Boston, 1891), 349–350. In view of President Theodore Roosevelt's well-known use of the term "muckrake" to rebuke writers who exposed social and economic abuses, it is interesting to find Phillips using the figure in a more exact sense—to stigmatize persons who were blind to the crying evil of his day. "We have seen," he declared in a speech in 1845, "the allegory of the muck rake of Bunyan made a reality by men of our times, who suffer the temptation of the sticks and straws beneath their feet to divert their eyes from the freeman's crown that hangs above their heads." Lorenzo Sears, *Wendell Phillips* (New York, 1909), 123.

11. As Garrison put it, "the ballot-box is not an anti-slavery, but a pro-slavery argument, so long as it is surrounded by the U. S. Constitution, which forbids all approach to it except on condition that the voter shall surrender fugitive slaves—suppress negro insurrections," etc. Garrisons, *Garrison*, III, 96.

12. The quoted phrase is from Charles Sumner in *The Commonwealth*, a Boston newspaper, March 28, 1851. Though the effect on the South was to exacerbate sectional relations, the Negro historian G. W. Williams believes that the Underground Railroad really acted as a "safety-valve to the institution of slavery. As soon as leaders arose among the slaves, refusing to endure the yoke, they came North." *History of the Negro Race in America* (New York, 1883), II, 59. Compare this view with the view of Northern abolitionists in regard to the American Colonization Society. While both Garrison and Phillips approved of the Underground Railroad, and a room above the *Liberator* office was used as a temporary refuge for runaways, Garrison regarded defiance of the Fugitive Slave Act as "no proof in itself of anti-slavery fidelity. That law is merely incidental to slavery, and there is no merit in opposition which extends no further than to its provisions. Our warfare is not against slave-hunting alone, but against the existence of slavery." Garrisons, *Garrison*, III, 365. W. H. Siebert, the leading authority, catalogued more than 3200 workers on the Underground, with

others still unidentified. For the basic work on the subject, see his *The Underground Railroad from Slavery to Freedom* (New York, 1899).

13. *Reminiscences* (Boston, 1899), 254.

14. J. F. Rhodes, *History of the United States* (New York, 1892–1919), II, 398. "Do you consider yourself an instrument in the hands of Providence?" one interviewer asked Brown, and the wounded prisoner answered, "I do." He added, "I don't think the people of the slave states will ever consider the subject of slavery in its true light till some other argument is resorted to than moral suasion." To someone who accused him of being fanatical, Brown replied, "I think you are fanatical. 'Whom the gods would destroy they first make mad,' and I think you are mad." *New York Herald*, October 21, 1859. The best biography is *John Brown* (Boston, 1910) by O. G. Villard, an admirer.

15. To such men Garrison wrathily retorted, "Has not the experience of two centuries shown that gradualism in theory is perpetuity in practice? . . . If the lapse of two hundred years be not sufficient to meet the claims of gradualism, (the rights of man out of the question), no quarter should longer be given to it by any friend of God or man." Garrisons, *Garrison*, II, 257. In fact, however, gradualism had in that period considerably enlarged the area of freedom in both the New World and the Old.

16. *Speeches and Letters* (*Everyman's Library*, London, 1907), 69. The wording in Mark, 3:25, is actually: "If a house be divided against itself, that house cannot stand."

17. *Speeches and Letters*, 195.

18. A. J. Beveridge, *Abraham Lincoln* (Boston, 1928), I, 194.

19. Lincoln's words in April 1865, as recalled by D. H. Chamberlain, later Governor of South Carolina, in the *New York Tribune*, November 4, 1883.

20. Korngold, *Two Friends of Man*, 315. As though to confirm this view, Garrison wrote in 1865 in the last issue of the *Liberator*, "To this day—such is the force of prejudice—there are multitudes who cannot be induced to read a single number of it, even on the score of curiosity, though their views on the slavery question are now precisely those it has uniformly advocated." Garrisons, *Garrison*, IV, 171.

21. *Speeches, Lectures, and Letters* (2d series), 448–449. Though James Russell Lowell once remarked that "Garrison is so used to standing alone that, like Daniel Boone, he moves away as the world creeps up to him, and goes farther *into the wilderness*," Garrison, in contrast to Phillips, understood and approved of Lincoln's cautious policy in regard to slavery. Defending Lincoln in the *Liberator* in 1864 he said, "His freedom to follow his convictions of duty as an individual is one thing—as the President of the United States, it is limited by the functions of his office; for the people do not elect a President to play the part of reformer or philanthropist, nor to enforce upon the nation his own peculiar ethical or humanitary ideas, without regard to his oath or their will. His primary and all-comprehensive duty is to maintain the Union and execute the Constitution, in good faith, according to the best of his ability, without reference to the views of any clique or party in the land, and for the general welfare." Lowell, *Letters* (C. E. Norton, ed., rev. ed., New York, 1904), I, 173; Garrisons, *Garrison*, IV, 119–120.

22. *Speeches and Letters*, 152.

23. Sears, *Phillips*, 204; Korngold, *Two Friends of Man*, 253; Rhodes, *History*, II, 409–415. Indeed, Emerson expressly complimented John Brown for rejecting "moral suasion" and believing "in his ideas to such an extent that he existed to put them all into action." "John Brown: Speech at Boston," *Works*, XI, 254. Garrison reconciled his nonresistance doctrines with Brown's violence by stating in the *Liberator*, "Our views of war and bloodshed, even in the best of causes, are too well known to need repeating here; but let no one who glories in the Revolutionary struggle of 1776 deny the right of slaves to imitate the example of our fathers." Garrisons, *Garrison*, III, 486.

24. "Lecture on the Times," *Works*, I, 263–264. As though repenting this sentiment of twenty years before, Emerson declared in an address on "Courage" during the Brown crisis, "I wish we might have health enough to know virtue when we see it, and not cry with fools 'madman' when a hero passes." But when he revised the speech for publication ten years later he omitted this passage. Rhodes, *History of the United States*, II, 413, 415.

25. "Slavery," *Works*, 735. For Southern expressions of the same view, see George Tucker, *Progress of the United States* (New York, 1843), 108–109, and C. B. Shaw's unsigned *A Reply to Professor Bledsoe* (Boston, 1857), 7.

26. Avery Craven, *The Coming of the Civil War* (New York, 1942), 152–153, further points out: "Long before the Northern attack on slavery required an answer, the situation at home demanded action. Serious agricultural depression, with resulting heavy emigration, combined with dissatisfaction over representation, the franchise, and inadequate transportation and educational facilities to produce, in areas where slaves were few, serious unrest and open censure of existing controls. . . . To check local aggression, even more than to meet Northern criticism, the pro-slavery argument was thus begun." See also Clement Eaton, *A History of the Old South* (New York, 1949), 384, and W. S. Jenkins, *Pro-Slavery Thought in the Old South* (Chapel Hill, 1935), 53–89, for the South's early militant pro-slavery attitude.

27. C. S. Sydnor, *The Development of Southern Sectionalism, 1819–1848* (Baton Rouge, 1948), 243.

28. For fuller expositions of this view, see Bernard De Voto, "The Easy Chair," *Harper's Magazine*, CXCII (1946), 123–126; A. M. Schlesinger, Jr., "The Causes of the Civil War," *Partisan Review*, XVI (1949), 969–981; and Pieter Geyl, *De Amerikaanse Burgeroorlog en het Probleem der Onvermijdelijkheid* (Koninklijke Nederlandse Akademie van Wetenschappen, *Mededelingen*, new series, XII, no. 5, 1949).

29. Garrisons, *Garrison*, III, 364.

30. "Thoreau," *Works* (Boston, 1892), I, 362.

31. Edward C. Delavan, Gerrit Smith and Francis Jackson were other prominent wealthy reformers in this period. A friend vainly warned Tappan "that philanthropic deeds and money-making were at war with each other. 'If a man of business is also a philanthropist,' said this person, 'he is in danger, while he is laying up treasure in heaven, of losing it on earth.' " Tappan, *Life of Arthur Tappan*, 64. For analyses of the financial support of abolitionism, consult Benjamin Quarles, "Sources of Abolitionist Income," *Mississippi Valley Historical Review*, XXXII

(1945–1946), 63–76, and Janet Wilson (James), "The Early Anti-Slavery Propaganda," *More Books,* XIX (1944), 400–404.

32. Though Communists upholding police-state tyranny are reactionaries rather than reformers in the American sense, the fact that some rich men and women have supported the American Communist party indicates again the dissociation of economic advantage and political conviction. For references to such aid, see James Oneal and G. A. Werner, *American Communism* (rev. ed., New York, 1947), 234, and the account in *Time,* January 9, 1950, p. 14, of Frederick Vanderbilt Field, great-great-grandson of Cornelius Vanderbilt, described as a financial "angel of Communism." On the Communists as reactionaries Justice Robert H. Jackson has recently observed, "The Communist program . . . . rejects the entire religious and cultural heritage of Western civilization, as well as the American economic and political systems. This Communist movement is a belated counter-revolution to the American Revolution, designed to undo the Declaration of Independence, the Constitution, and our Bill of Rights, and overturn our system of free, representative self-government." Jackson's opinion in American Communications Association *et al. v.* Douds, and United Steelworkers *et al. v.* National Labor Relations Board, May 8, 1950. As to the Communist attitude toward reform Joseph Stalin himself has written, "The revolutionary will accept a reform in order to use it as a screen behind which his illegal activities for the revolutionary preparation of the masses for the overthrow of the bourgeoisie may be intensified." *Foundations of Leninism* (New York, 1932), 103.

33. W. A. White, *Calvin Coolidge* (New York, 1925), 218. As E. R. A. Seligman observes in *The Economic Interpretation of History* (New York, 1902), 126, "History is full of examples where nations, like individuals, have acted unselfishly and have followed the generous promptings of the higher life. The ethical and the religious teachers have not worked in vain." He goes on to say "that the conception of morality is a social product" and hence "that pure ethical or religious idealism has made itself felt only within the limitations of existing economic conditions."

34. The quotation is from the Democratic platform of 1900. G. D. Ellis, comp., *Platforms of the Two Great Parties* (Washington, 1920), 105.

35. The Whittier characterization is from Edwin Markham, quoted in Albert Mordell, *Quaker Militant, John Greenleaf Whittier* (Boston, 1933), p. viii; and the reference to Mrs. Stowe, from Edward Channing, *A History of the United States* (New York, 1905–1925), VI, 113. See L. D. Turner, "Anti-Slavery Sentiment in American Literature," *Journal of Negro History*, XIV (1929), 371–492, for a survey of that subject from colonial times, and A. M. Schlesinger, Jr., *The Age of Jackson* (Boston, 1945), chap. xxix, for the literary support of Jacksonian political reform. Novels in this tradition of social and political protest excite the anger of reactionaries on the extreme left as well as on the extreme right. Thus *Pravda* of Prague, Czechoslovakia, in an article calling for "More Vigilance on the Cultural Front," flayed *The Grapes of Wrath* because it "served the cause of capitalism by its 'social sympathies,' since it demanded measures against the proletarianization of land, and the agricultural laws which were then enacted were designed to avert the danger that the oppressed would organize themselves collectively." John MacCormac, "Reading by Red Star Light," *Saturday Review of Literature*, XXXIII, no. 8 (February 25, 1950), 9.

36. *Protestant Jesuitism* (New York, 1836), 53–54, written anonymously by Calvin Colton, who regarded such bodies disapprovingly.

37. "Mr. Churchill and Me-Tooism," *Boston Globe*, January 26, 1950. Herbert Agar presents the same thesis in *The Price of Union* (Boston, 1950).

38. K. C. MacKay, *The Progressive Movement of 1924* (New York, 1947), estimates that La Follette polled somewhat more than half his strength from the farmers.

39. The older and weaker party was the Socialist Labor party. Until the ultimate goal is reached, the Socialist party has always urged a long list of timely reforms—such as woman suffrage, a graduated income tax and social security—which have attracted bourgeois liberals. For example, compare the dues-paying membership of 108,000 in 1919 with the vote polled by the Socialist

ticket in the next year's election. H. W. Laidler, *Social-Economic Movements* (New York, 1944), 591.

40. The Communist ticket in 1940 polled 49,000 votes. The party membership in 1950 was 55,000, according to J. Edgar Hoover, director of the FBI. *New York Times*, May 3, 1950.

41. To some extent La Follette's Progressives in 1924 and Wallace's Progressives in 1948 were also chips respectively off the Republican and Democratic parties.

42. In addition, three splinter parties have captured electoral votes: the Liberal Republicans in 1872, in combination with the Democrats; the Progressives in 1912; and the Dixiecrats (the States' Rights party) in 1948. Theodore Roosevelt would not run a second time on the Progressive ticket because he said the voters were naturally Republicans or Democrats. *Works* (New York, 1923–1926), XXIV, 416.

43. J. D. Hicks believes that "in possibly half a dozen instances the third party vote has snatched victory from one major party ticket to give it to the other." "The Third Party Tradition in American Politics," *Mississippi Valley Historical Review*, XX (1933–1934), 26. It is only fair to note that the Prohibition vote in 1884 is often credited in this manner with defeating Blaine in New York and thus bringing into the White House Grover Cleveland, the champion of clean government, a low tariff and civil-service reform; but the Mugwump revolt of independent Republicans was probably the more decisive factor. See A. M. Schlesinger, *The Rise of the City* (New York, 1933), 400–401.

44. Most of the states had taken similar action earlier, the Massachusetts statute dating from 1890 and Wisconsin's from 1899.

III. THE REVOLT AGAINST REVOLT

1. "Lecture on the Times," *Works* (Boston, 1883–1887), I, 255.

2. Thomas Hamilton, *Men and Manners in America* (London, 1833), I, 131.

3. *Works* (Boston, 1892), VI, 36.

4. *Recollections of a Busy Life* (New York, 1868), 515–516.

5. Roosevelt, *Autobiography* (New York, 1913), 206; Lowell, "Thoreau," *Works*, I, 363. For a trenchant arraignment of "social quackery" by one who regarded all reformers as quacks, see William Graham Sumner's chapter "On the Value, as a Sociological Principle, of the Rule to Mind One's Own Business" in *What Social Classes Owe to Each Other* (New York, 1883).

6. Federal Writers' Project, *Massachusetts* (Boston, 1937), 149. In 1947, when a group of distinguished citizens asked Governor Robert Bradford of Massachusetts to accept a plaque in honor of Sacco and Vanzetti, who had been executed twenty years before under circumstances making impossible a fair trial, he replied that public opinion in the Commonwealth was not yet ready for such action. G. L. Joughin and E. M. Morgan, *The Legacy of Sacco and Vanzetti* (New York, 1948), p. xiv.

7. The version given here is an abbreviation of the original, which may be found in *The Clocks of Rondaine and Other Stories* (New York, 1892), 1–23.

8. *Works*, VI, 18.

9. The two sentences are quoted from Peter Force, comp., *American Archives* (4th series, Washington, 1837–1846), I, 1188; V, 1141–1142. For fuller elucidations of the Tory attitude, consult L. W. Labaree, "The Nature of American Loyalism," American Antiquarian Society, *Proceedings*, LIV (1945), 15–58, and M. C. Tyler, *The Literary History of the American Revolution* (New York, 1897), I, chaps. xii–xviii, xxii; II, chaps. xxvii–xxix.

10. This discussion is based on C. E. Merriam, *A History of American Political Theories* (New York, 1903), 187–191, and J. B. McMaster, *A History of the People of the United States* (New York, 1883–1913), V, 376–394.

11. An important documentary source is *Cotton Is King, and Pro-Slavery Arguments* (Augusta, 1860), edited by E. N. Elliott, president of Planters' College, Mississippi. W. S. Jenkins, *Pro-Slavery Thought in the Old South* (Chapel Hill, 1935), is an excellent digest, and D. A. Hartman, "The Psychological Point of View in History: Some Phases of the Slavery Struggle," *Journal of Abnormal Psychology and Social Psychology*, XVII (1922), 261–273, offers a psychological explanation.

12. Jenkins, *Pro-Slavery Thought*, 286. For further discussion,

see R. H. Taylor, "The Mud-Sill Theory in South Carolina," South Carolina Historical Association, *Proceedings for 1939,* 35–43.

13. The editorial is reprinted in J. R. Commons and others, eds., *Documentary History of American Industrial Society* (Cleveland, 1909–1911), V, 105, from the *National Gazette,* July 1830. For the Rhode Island protest, see F. T. Carlton, *Economic Influences upon Educational Progress in the United States, 1820–1850* (Madison, 1908), 61–62. The other objections are summarized in E. P. Cubberley, *Public Education in the United States* (rev. ed., Boston, 1934), 166, and Merle Curti, *The Social Ideas of American Educators* (New York, 1935), 87–88.

14. All the quotations on the income-tax issue are from Sidney Ratner, *American Taxation* (New York, 1942), 200, 203, 213.

15. Ratner, *American Taxation,* 260.

16. Editorial by Frank I. Cobb in the *New York World,* January 1912, reprinted in the *New York Herald Tribune,* December 31, 1937.

17. W. P. and F. J. Garrison, *William Lloyd Garrison* (New York, 1885–1889), I, 336; III, 32–33; and, for the Southern counterblast, Avery Craven, *The Coming of the Civil War* (New York, 1942), 156, 173–174. A. A. Roback has compiled *A Dictionary of International Slurs* (Cambridge, 1944).

18. Quoted in President Truman's Jefferson-Jackson Day address, *New York Times,* January 17, 1950.

19. *New York Times,* February 7, 1950. As Representative Martin put it, "the road down which we are headed . . . terminates in socialism, whether you call it welfare state, collectivism or by some other name just as meaningless" (*ibid.,* February 22), and George Minot, editorializing on the welfare state in the *Boston Herald,* February 26, chorused, "You can call it anything you like—communism, statism, the square, the new, the raw or the fair deal—but it all adds up to Socialism." To the Republican National Committee's definition of the issue Oscar E. Ewing, Federal Security Administrator, replied on behalf of the administration, "What kind of a political slogan is that? Do they mean that only a Republican is dedicated to liberty in America?

Do they dare to say that American liberals, who have produced men like Roosevelt and Truman and Hillman, do not know the value of individual liberty, of human dignity, of American freedom? And as for socialism—at a time when American industry is a hundred times healthier than at any point during the last years of the last Republican administration, these lackwit leaders of reaction presume to raise the scarecrow of socialism." *New York Times*, March 12, 1950.

20. *New York Times*, February 11, 1950; *Time*, LV, no. 8 (February 20, 1950), 17.

21. "Fragment. On Government" (1854), *Complete Works* (J. G. Nicolay and John Hay, eds., rev. ed., New York, 1905), II, 186–187.

22. D. D. McKean, *Party and Pressure Politics* (Boston, 1949), 659. For further historical light on the concept, read A. M. Schlesinger, Jr., " 'The Welfare State,' " *Reporter*, I, no. 13 (October 10, 1949), 28–30. As the Democratic Senator Herbert H. Lehman of New York put it, "In my opinion, men of little vision have lost sight of the most important truth of our times— that a government which has secured the greatest degree of welfare for its people is the government which stands most firmly against totalitarianism." *New York Times*, April 16, 1950.

23. Thus an editorial in the conservative *Boston Herald*, January 22, 1950, began, "The issue between the Democratic and the Republican parties of the United States is not one that involves the 'welfare state' as a political objective. . . . The issue . . . is . . . but the means of attainment." By the same token, the identical Republican National Committee which phrased the issue as "liberty against socialism" went on to say, "We hold that the Government can use its just powers to foster national health, promote real security for the aged, develop sound agricultural and labor-management policies and advance civil rights." *New York Times*, February 7, 1950.

24. R. A. Billington, *The Protestant Crusade, 1800–1860* (New York, 1938), 384–385; G. D. Ellis, comp., *Platforms of the Two Great Parties* (Washington, 1920), 7–8.

25. James Oneal and G. W. Werner, *American Communism* (rev. ed., New York, 1947), 274, 283. Of "The Klan's Fight for

Americanism," Imperial Wizard H. W. Evans wrote in the *North American Review*, CCXXIII (1926), 58, "The textbooks have been so perverted that Americanism is falsified, distorted and betrayed."

26. For references to all these groups, see Arthur Derounian ("John Roy Carlson"), *Under Cover* (New York, 1943).

27. H. D. Gideonse, "Changing Issues in Academic Freedom," American Philosophical Society, *Proceedings*, XCIV (1950), 99. For other information about the Committee, turn to William Gellermann, *Martin Dies* (New York, 1944), and A. R. Ogden, *The Dies Committee* (rev. ed., Washington, 1945).

28. Jonathan Swift, *Gulliver's Travels and Selected Writings in Prose and Verse* (John Hayward, ed., New York, 1934), 53–54.

29. *New York Times*, February 18, March 18, 1950.

30. "We Must Not Be Afraid of Change," *New York Times Magazine*, April 3, 1949, an article to which the next two paragraphs are also indebted. In similar vein Justice Robert H. Jackson has remarked, "Nothing is more pernicious than the idea that every radical measure is 'Communistic' or every liberal-minded person a 'Communist.' One of the tragedies of our time is the confusion between reform and Communism—a confusion to which both the friends and enemies of reform have contributed, the one by failing to take a clear stand against Communists and Communism and the other by characterizing even the most moderate suggestion of reform as 'Communistic' and its advocates as 'Communists.'" Jackson's opinion in American Communications Association *et al. v.* Douds, and United Steelworkers *et al. v.* National Labor Relations Board, May 8, 1950.

31. Norman Foerster in *New York Times*, February 19, 1950.

32. E. J. McGrath in his annual report, *New York Times*, February 9, 1950.

33. "Thoreau," *Works*, I, 364.

34. Ralph Korngold, *Two Friends of Man* (Boston, 1950), 182.

INDEX

INDEX

Abolitionism, in England and America compared, 5–6; aided by persecution, 11; and churches, 14; and Declaration of Independence, 16; wars help, 18; as regarded in South, 20, 42–44; in East and West, 20–21; as state issue, 22; achieved, 23, 39, 45; schools of, 31–42; as cause of Civil War, 44; in other lands, 45; in relation to capitalism, 45–46; economic motivation for, 49–50; literature on, 51; in election of 1844, 59; arguments against, 76–77; financial support of, 111–112

Adams, John, on foes of independence, 74; opposes male suffrage, 75

Age of Enlightenment, influences America, 15

Alcott, Bronson, on clergy, 13, 103

America First Committee, during World War II, 89

American and Americanism, as historical terms, 87–90

American Anti-Slavery Society, formed, 6; rift in, 38

American Colonization Society, career of, 106–107

American party, aims of, 87

American Protective Association, patrioteering methods of, 88

American Revolution, and clergy, 12–13; helps reform, 18; opposed, 74; sloganeering in, 82

Antin, Mary, on Declaration of Independence, 16–17

Antislavery. See Abolitionism

Baldwin, Roger, arrested, 16

Ballou, Adin, defends nonresistance, 107

Beecher, H. W., on Garrison, 44

Bellamy, Edward, as author, 51

Bibliography, 99–102

Birney, J. B., as gradualist, 38, 43

Boston Herald, on federal subsidies, 106; on welfare state, 116, 117

Bradford, Robert, rejects plaque, 115

Brown, John, career of, 36–37; Northern reaction to, 41–42, 110; Southern reaction to, 42; interviewed, 109

Bryan, W. J., 49; appeals to religion, 14–15

Bryce, James, on federalism, 21–22, 104; on religion and reform, 103

Burke, Edmund, 5; on Protestantism, 12

Capitalism, and Negro emancipation, 45–46